ARTIST INDEX

CONTENTS

VOLUME 2 • CLASSIC ROCK TO MODERN ROCK | *easy* GUITAR TAB EDITION

Rolling Stone

GUITAR CLASSICS VOLUME 2 • CLASSIC ROCK TO MODERN ROCK

67 SELECTIONS FROM THE

500 GREATEST SONGS OF ALL TIME

Alfred Publishing Co., Inc.
16320 Roscoe Blvd., Suite 100
P.O. Box 10003
Van Nuys, CA 91410-0003
alfred.com

Rolling Stone® 500 Greatest Songs of All Time

Welcome to the ultimate jukebox: the *Rolling Stone* 500, a celebration of the greatest rock & roll songs of all time, chosen by a five-star jury of singers, musicians, producers, industry figures, critics and, of course, songwriters. The editors of *Rolling Stone* called on rock stars and leading authorities to list their fifty favorite songs, in order of preference. The 172 voters, who included Brian Wilson, Joni Mitchell and Wilco's Jeff Tweedy, were asked to select songs from the rock & roll era. They nominated 2,103 songs in virtually every pop-music genre of the past half-century and beyond, from Hank Williams to OutKast. The results were tabulated according to a weighted point system.

For this *RS* 500, the word *song* refers to both a composition and its definitive recorded performance, as a single or an album track. Bob Dylan, the Beatles and the Rolling Stones accounted for a combined total of 117 nominated songs, a measure of their unbroken reign as rock's most influential, beloved artists. Nirvana and the Clash crashed the top twenty, rubbing guitars with Chuck Berry and Jimi Hendrix.

This *RS* 500 is also a tribute to the eternal power of popular music, and great songwriting in particular, to reflect and transform the times in which we hear it. The *RS* 500 salutes the songs that move us—and the artists who create them. It is also proof that whenever you want to know what's going on, listen to the music.

CONTENTS

Alison
Elvis Costello

Written by: Costello
Produced by: Nick Lowe
Released: Nov. '77 on Columbia
Charts: did not chart

▶▶**No. 318** *from Rolling Stone® Magazine's 500 Greatest Songs of All Time*

Some people think "Alison" is a murder ballad. "It isn't," Costello told *Rolling Stone* in 2002. "It's about disappointing somebody. It's a thin line between love and hate, as the Persuaders sang." Contrary to myth, the backup band was *not* Huey Lewis and the News.

Appears on: My Aim Is True (Rhino)

(Music appears on page 20)

Another Brick in the Wall Part 2
Pink Floyd

Written by: Roger Waters
Produced by: Bob Ezrin, Waters, David Gilmour
Released: Nov. '79 on Columbia
Charts: 25 weeks; top spot no. 1

▶▶**No. 375** *from Rolling Stone® Magazine's 500 Greatest Songs of All Time*

Waters' vicious attack on teachers who practice "dark sarcasm in the classroom" was inspired by the cruelty of his own schoolmasters. "The school I was at – they were really like that," Waters said. "They were so fucked up, [all] they had to offer was their own bitterness and cynicism." "Another Brick" is rendered in three versions on *The Wall*, but "Part 2" was the hit.

Appears on: The Wall (Capitol)

(Music appears on page 24)

Back in Black
AC/DC

Written by: Angus Young, Malcolm Young, Brian Johnson
Produced by: Mutt Lange
Released: July '80 on Atlantic
Charts: 15 weeks; top spot no. 37

▶▶**No. 187** *from Rolling Stone® Magazine's 500 Greatest Songs of All Time*

One week in 1980, Angus and Malcolm Young were running through ideas with frontman Bon Scott in a London rehearsal studio. The next Tuesday, Scott drank himself to death. Instead of retreating, the Youngs finished the songs with a new singer, Brian Johnson. "Malcolm asked me if this riff he had was too funky," says Angus. "And I said, 'Well, if you're gonna discard it, give it to me!'"

Appears on: Back in Black (Sony)

(Music appears on page 29)

Bad Moon Rising
Creedence Clearwater Revival

Written by: John Fogerty
Produced by: Fogerty
Released: April '69 on Fantasy
Charts: 14 weeks; top spot no. 2

▶▶**No. 355** *from Rolling Stone® Magazine's 500 Greatest Songs of All Time*

With violence at home and a war abroad, there really was a bad moon on the rise. "Bad Moon Rising" had one of CCR's catchiest swamp-rock guitar riffs.

Appears on: Green River (Fantasy)

(Music appears on page 36)

Beat It
Michael Jackson

Written by: Jackson
Produced by: Quincy Jones
Released: Dec. '82 on Epic
Charts: 25 weeks; top spot no. 1

▶▶**No. 337** *from Rolling Stone® Magazine's 500 Greatest Songs of All Time*

"I wanted to write the type of rock song that I would go out and buy," said Jackson, "but also something totally different from the rock music I was hearing on Top Forty radio." The result was a throbbing dance single with a watch-my-fingers-fly guitar solo provided by Eddie Van Halen.

Appears on: Thriller (Epic)

(Music appears on page 39)

Billie Jean
Michael Jackson

Written by: Jackson
Produced by: Jackson, Quincy Jones
Released: Jan. '83 on Epic
Charts: 7 weeks; top spot no. 1

▶▶**No. 58** *from Rolling Stone® Magazine's 500 Greatest Songs of All Time*

Sinuous, paranoid and omnipresent: the single that made Jackson the biggest star since Elvis was a denial of a paternity suit, and it spent seven weeks at Number One. Jackson came up with the irresistible rhythm track on his home drum machine and nailed the vocals in one take. "I knew it was going to be big while I was writing it," he said. "I was really absorbed in writing it." How absorbed? He was thinking about the song while riding in his Rolls down the Ventura Freeway in California – and didn't notice the car was on fire.

Appears on: Thriller (Sony)

(Music appears on page 46)

Bitter Sweet Symphony
The Verve

Written by: Mick Jagger, Keith Richards, Richard Ashcroft
Produced by: The Verve, Christopher Marc Potter, Youth
Released: Sept. '97 on Virgin
Charts: 20 weeks; top spot no. 12

》》**No. 382** *from Rolling Stone® Magazine's 500 Greatest Songs of All Time*

Bittersweet, indeed. Since it used a sample from an orchestral version of a Rolling Stones song, the Verve hit was credited to Jagger-Richards. Ashcroft claimed it was the best song the Stones had written in twenty years.

Appears on: Urban Hymns (Virgin)

(Music appears on page 52)

Bizarre Love Triangle
New Order

Written by: Bernard Albrecht, Gillian Gilbert, Peter Hook, Stephen Morris
Produced by: New Order
Released: Oct. '86 on Qwest
Charts: 2 weeks; top spot no. 98

》》**No. 201** *from Rolling Stone® Magazine's 500 Greatest Songs of All Time*

After the death of Joy Division's Ian Curtis, his bandmates became New Order. "There's life and there's death," drummer Morris said in 1983. "We were still alive, so we thought we'd carry on doing it." New Order wrote their moody synth-pop hits in a Manchester rehearsal room next to a cemetery. Said Morris, "Fate writes the lyrics, and we do the rest."

Appears on: Substance (Qwest)

(Music appears on page 62)

Black Dog
Led Zeppelin

Written by: Jimmy Page, Robert Plant, John Paul Jones
Produced by: Page
Released: Nov. '71 on Atlantic
Charts: 12 weeks; top spot no. 15

》》**No. 294** *from Rolling Stone® Magazine's 500 Greatest Songs of All Time*

A dog meandering the grounds outside Zeppelin's studio in rural England inspired the title, but the subject was honeydripping sex. "Things like 'Black Dog' are blatant let's-do-it-in-the-bath-type things," Plant said, "but they make their point."

Appears on: Led Zeppelin IV (Atlantic)

(Music appears on page 55)

Blitzkrieg Bop
Ramones

Written by: Ramones
Produced by: Craig Leon
Released: May '76 on Sire
Charts: did not chart

》》**No. 92** *from Rolling Stone® Magazine's 500 Greatest Songs of All Time*

In less than three minutes, this song threw down the blueprint for punk rock. It's all here on the opening track of the Ramones' debut: the buzz-saw chords, which Johnny played on his fifty-dollar Mosrite guitar; the snotty words, courtesy of drummer Tommy (with bassist Dee Dee adding the brilliant line "Shoot 'em in the back now"); and the hairball-in-the-throat vocals, sung by Joey in a faux-British accent. Recorded on the cheap at New York's Radio City Music Hall, of all places, "Blitzkrieg Bop" never made the charts; instead, it almost single-handedly created a world beyond the charts.

Appears on: Ramones (Rhino)

(Music appears on page 66)

Born in the U.S.A.
Bruce Springsteen

Written by: Springsteen
Produced by: Springsteen, Jon Landau, Chuck Plotkin, Steve Van Zandt
Released: June '84 on Columbia
Charts: 17 weeks; top spot no. 9

》》**No. 275** *from Rolling Stone® Magazine's 500 Greatest Songs of All Time*

Before it became the centerpiece of Springsteen's biggest album, "U.S.A." was an acoustic protest song meant for *Nebraska*. But when Springsteen revived it with the E Street Band, Roy Bittan came up with a monster synth riff and Max Weinberg hammered out a beat like he was using M-80s for drumsticks. "We played it two times, and our second take is the record," Springsteen said. "That thing in the end with all the drums, that just kinda happened."

Appears on: Born in the U.S.A. (Columbia)

(Music appears on page 68)

Born to Run
Bruce Springsteen

Written by: Springsteen
Produced by: Springsteen, Mike Appel
Released: Aug. '75 on Columbia
Charts: 11 weeks; top spot no. 23

》》**No. 21** *from Rolling Stone® Magazine's 500 Greatest Songs of All Time*

This song's four and a half minutes took three and a half months to cut. Aiming for the impact of Phil Spector's Wall of Sound, Springsteen included strings, glockenspiel, multiple keyboards – and more than a dozen guitar tracks. The words poured out just as relentlessly, telling a story of young lovers on the highways of New Jersey. "I don't know how important the settings are in the first place," Springsteen told *Rolling Stone*. "It's the idea behind the settings. It could be New Jersey, it could be California, it could be Alaska."

Appears on: Born to Run (Columbia)

(Music appears on page 70)

The Boys of Summer
Don Henley

Written by: Henley, Mike Campbell
Produced by: Henley, Campbell, Danny Kortchmar, Greg Ladanyi
Released: Nov. '84 on Geffen
Charts: 22 weeks; top spot no. 5
»**No. 416** *from Rolling Stone® Magazine's 500 Greatest Songs of All Time*

Henley gave California rock a stylish Eighties makeover with this poignant lament for his generation, featuring the famous line "Out on the road today/I saw a Deadhead sticker on a Cadillac." When the Ataris did their hit punk-rock cover version in 2003, they changed it to a Black Flag sticker – but the sentiment was the same.

Appears on: Building the Perfect Beast (Geffen)

(Music appears on page 76)

Brown Sugar
The Rolling Stones

Written by: Mick Jagger, Keith Richards
Produced by: Jimmy Miller
Released: April '71 on Rolling Stones
Charts: 12 weeks; top spot no. 1
»**No. 490** *from Rolling Stone® Magazine's 500 Greatest Songs of All Time*

Here the Stones lay waste to a battery of taboo topics – slavery, sadomasochism, interracial sex – and still manage to be catchy as hell. The song got its start at a session at Muscle Shoals studios: Jagger scrawled three verses on a stenographer's pad, and Richards followed with an impossibly raunchy riff. Add some exultant punctuations ("Yeah! Yeah! *Woooo*!") and you have a Stones concert staple.

Appears on: Sticky Fingers (Virgin)

(Music appears on page 82)

Come Together
The Beatles

Written by: John Lennon, Paul McCartney
Produced by: George Martin
Released: Sept. '69 on Apple
Charts: 16 weeks; top spot no. 1
»**No. 202** *from Rolling Stone® Magazine's 500 Greatest Songs of All Time*

Timothy Leary was running for governor of California when he asked Lennon to write a campaign song for him. The resulting tune was not politically useful, so Lennon brought it to the *Abbey Road* sessions. Recalled McCartney, "I said, 'Let's slow it down with a swampy bass-and-drums vibe.' I came up with a bass line, and it all flowed from there." It was the last time all four Beatles cut a song together.

Appears on: Abbey Road (Apple)

(Music appears on page 94)

Comfortably Numb
Pink Floyd

Written by: David Gilmour, Roger Waters
Produced by: Bob Ezrin
Released: Dec. '79 on Columbia
Charts: did not chart
»**No. 314** *from Rolling Stone® Magazine's 500 Greatest Songs of All Time*

Waters based one of the saddest drug songs ever written on a sleazy Philadelphia doctor who injected him with tranquilizers before a gig when he was suffering from hepatitis. "That was the longest two hours of my life," Waters said. "Trying to do a show when you can hardly lift your arm."

Appears on: The Wall (Capitol)

(Music appears on page 89)

Fake Plastic Trees
Radiohead

Written by: Radiohead
Produced by: John Leckie
Released: March '95 on Capitol
Charts: 4 weeks; top spot no. 65
»**No. 376** *from Rolling Stone® Magazine's 500 Greatest Songs of All Time*

Radiohead frontman Thom Yorke would describe "Fake Plastic Trees" as the song on which he found his lyrical voice. He cut the vocal, accompanying himself on acoustic guitar, in one take, then the band filled in its parts around him. Yorke said the song began as "a very nice melody which I had no idea what to do with, then you wake up and find your head singing some words to it."

Appears on: The Bends (Capitol)

(Music appears on page 100)

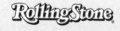

Family Affair
Sly and the Family Stone

Written by: Sylvester Stewart (Sly Stone)
Produced by: Stone
Released: Oct. '71 on Epic
Charts: 14 weeks; top spot no. 1

»No. 138 *from Rolling Stone® Magazine's 500 Greatest Songs of All Time*

When "There's a Riot Goin' On" came out in 1971, a *Rolling Stone* reporter mentioned the rumor that Sly Stone had played all the instruments himself, and he asked Sly just how much he played. "I've forgotten, man," Stone said. "Whatever was left." The leadoff single, the aquatic funk number "Family Affair," was widely considered to be about his relationships with his band, family and the Black Panthers. "Well, I'll tell ya," Stone said, "they may be trying to tear me apart; I don't feel it. Song's not about *that*. Song's about *a* family affair, whether it's a result of genetic processes or a situation in the environment."

Appears on: There's a Riot Goin' On (Sony)

(Music appears on page 102)

Fast Car
Tracy Chapman

Written by: Chapman
Produced by: David Kershenbaum
Released: April '88 on Elektra
Charts: 21 weeks; top spot no. 6

»No. 165 *from Rolling Stone® Magazine's 500 Greatest Songs of All Time*

Tracy Chapman was a hardened veteran of Boston coffeehouse gigs (she once got a demotape rejection letter suggesting she tune her guitar) when a classmate at Tufts University told his music-publisher dad to check her out. Soon after, she made her 1988 debut, featuring this haunting meditation on escape. "Fast Car" won a Grammy, setting Chapman's career in motion.

Appears on: Tracy Chapman (Elektra)

(Music appears on page 106)

Get Up (I Feel Like Being a) Sex Machine
James Brown

Written by: Brown, Bobby Byrd, Ron Lenhoff
Produced by: Brown
Released: July '70 on King
Charts: 9 weeks; top spot no. 15

»No. 326 *from Rolling Stone® Magazine's 500 Greatest Songs of All Time*

Engineer Lenhoff got co-writing credit for this funk monument, mostly because he got out of bed and

drove five hours to Nashville to record this duet with ex-Famous Flame Byrd, which Brown insisted must be cut pronto.

Appears on: 50th Anniversary Collection (UTV/Polydor)

(Music appears on page 111)

Gimme Shelter
The Rolling Stones

Written by: Mick Jagger, Keith Richards
Produced by: Jimmy Miller
Released: April '69 on London
Charts: 11 weeks; top spot no. 21

»No. 38 *from Rolling Stone® Magazine's 500 Greatest Songs of All Time*

Richards' opening, strummed on an electric-acoustic guitar modeled after a Chuck Berry favorite, conjures an aura of dread unparalleled in the Stones canon. Then singer Merry Clayton brings down the apocalypse with a soul-racked wail: "Oh, murder, it's just a shot away." The song surfaced within days of Meredith Hunter's murder at Altamont.

Appears on: Let It Bleed (Abkco)

(Music appears on page 116)

Go Your Own Way
Fleetwood Mac

Written by: Lindsey Buckingham
Produced by: Fleetwood Mac, Richard Dashut, Ken Caillat
Released: Jan. '77 on Warner Bros.
Charts: 15 weeks; top spot no. 10

»No. 119 *from Rolling Stone® Magazine's 500 Greatest Songs of All Time*

Quintessential Fleetwood Mac: "I very much resented him telling the world that 'packing up, shacking up' with different men was all I wanted to do," said Stevie Nicks of this Buckingham kiss-off.

Appears on: Rumours (Warner Bros.)

(Music appears on page 128)

God Save the Queen
The Sex Pistols

Written by: Johnny Rotten, Steve Jones, Glen Matlock, Paul Cook
Produced by: Chris Thomas
Released: May '77 on Warner Bros.
Charts: did not chart

»No. 173 *from Rolling Stone® Magazine's 500 Greatest Songs of All Time*

Banned by the BBC for "gross bad taste," this blast of nihilism savaged the pomp of Queen Elizabeth II's silver jubilee and came in a sleeve showing Her Majesty with a safety pin through her lip. "Watching her on

telly, as far as I'm concerned, she ain't no human being," sneered singer Johnny Rotten. "She's a piece of cardboard they drag around on a trolley."

Appears on: Never Mind the Bollocks, Here's the Sex Pistols (Warner Bros.)

(Music appears on page 132)

Good Times
Chic

Written by: Nile Rodgers, Bernard Edwards
Produced by: Rodgers, Edwards
Released: June '79 on Atlantic
Charts: 19 weeks; top spot no. 1
»No. 224 *from Rolling Stone® Magazine's 500 Greatest Songs of All Time*

The tone was half-ironic when Chic released "Good Times," a hedonistic roller-disco tune, during the Seventies recession. The other half was pure joy, and Edwards' bass line – bouncing on one note, then climbing – proved too snappy for just one song. Queen borrowed it for "Another One Bites the Dust"; in the South Bronx, the Sugarhill Gang put it under "Rappers Delight."

Appears on: Risqué (Atlantic)

(Music appears on page 138)

Graceland
Paul Simon

Written by: Simon
Produced by: Simon
Released: Sept. '86 on Warner Bros.
Charts: 7 weeks; top spot no. 81
»No. 485 *from Rolling Stone® Magazine's 500 Greatest Songs of All Time*

Simon recorded "Graceland" with South African mbaqanga musicians; he also got backup harmonies from his heroes, the Everly Brothers. But he didn't think of "Graceland" as the album's title song until late in the process. "I thought it was distracting," he said. "I figured people would think I'm writing about Elvis Presley, and this is a South African record."

Appears on: Graceland (Rhino)

(Music appears on page 121)

Heartbreaker
Led Zeppelin

Written by: Jimmy Page, Robert Plant, John Bonham, John Paul Jones
Produced by: Page
Released: Oct. '69 on Atlantic
Charts: non-single
»No. 320 *from Rolling Stone® Magazine's 500 Greatest Songs of All Time*

"Heartbreaker," like much of *Led Zeppelin II*, was

recorded hit-and-run style on Zep's 1969 American tour. The awesome swagger captures the debauched mood of the band's wild early days in L.A. "Nineteen years old and never been kissed," Plant recalled in 1975. "I remember it well. It's been a long time. Nowadays we're more into staying in our room and reading Nietzsche."

Appears on: Led Zeppelin II (Atlantic)

(Music appears on page 140)

Highway to Hell
AC/DC

Written by: Angus Young, Malcolm Young, Bon Scott
Produced by: Robert John Lange
Released: Aug. '79 on Atlantic
Charts: 10 weeks; top spot no. 47
»No. 254 *from Rolling Stone® Magazine's 500 Greatest Songs of All Time*

"I've been on the road for thirteen years," AC/DC singer Scott said in 1978. "Planes, hotels, groupies, booze … they all scrape something from you." Pumped up by producer Lange, "Highway" is the last will and testament of Scott: When he yells, "Don't stop me," right before Angus Young's guitar solo, it's clear that no one could – he drank himself to death in 1980.

Appears on: Highway to Hell (Atlantic)

(Music appears on page 156)

Hotel California
Eagles

Written by: Don Felder, Glenn Frey, Don Henley
Produced by: Bill Szymczyk
Released: Dec. '76 on Asylum
Charts: 19 weeks; top spot no. 1
»No. 49 *from Rolling Stone® Magazine's 500 Greatest Songs of All Time*

"Hotel California" was rumored to be about heroin addiction or Satan worship, but Henley had more prosaic things on his mind: "We were all middle-class kids from the Midwest," he said. "'Hotel California' was our interpretation of the high life in Los Angeles." (That doesn't preclude heroin or Satan.) A problem arose when the band, recording in Miami, was unable to re-create Felder's twelve-string intro and twin-guitar coda. Panicked, Felder called his housekeeper in L.A. and sent her digging through tapes in his home studio so she could play his demo back over the phone.

Appears on: Hotel California (Elektra)

(Music appears on page 160)

I Wanna Be Sedated
Ramones

Written by: Ramones
Produced by: Tommy Erdelyi, Ed Stasium
Released: Oct. '78 on Sire
Charts: did not chart
»No. 144 *from Rolling Stone® Magazine's 500 Greatest Songs of All Time*

The greatest god-does-the-road-ever-suck song, "I Wanna Be Sedated" was written by Joey Ramone, who at the time was suffering from severe teakettle burns and had to fly to London for a gig. Plagued by obsessive-compulsive disorder and various other ailments, Joey always had a rough time touring. "Put me in a wheelchair/And get me to the show/Hurry hurry hurry/Before I go loco!" he rants. The sound is equally pissed-off: Johnny's guitar solo – the same note, sixty-five times in a row – is the ultimate expression of his anti-artifice philosophy; the bubblegum-pop key change that follows it, though, is pure Joey.

Appears on: Road to Ruin (Rhino)

(Music appears on page 170)

Into the Mystic
Van Morrison

Written by: Morrison
Produced by: Morrison
Released: March '70 on Warner Bros.
Charts: non-single
»No. 480 *from Rolling Stone® Magazine's 500 Greatest Songs of All Time*

"Into the Mystic" is one of Morrison's warmest ballads, an Otis Redding-style reverie with acoustic guitar and horns. The lyrics are truly mysterious: "People say, 'What does this mean?'" said Morrison. "A lot of times I have no idea what I mean. That's what I like about rock & roll – the concept. Like Little Richard – what does he mean? You can't take him apart; that's rock & roll to me."

Appears on: Moondance (Warner Bros.)

(Music appears on page 174)

Iron Man
Black Sabbath

Written by: Black Sabbath
Produced by: Roger Bain
Released: Feb. '71 on Warner
Charts: 10 weeks; top spot no. 52
»No. 310 *from Rolling Stone® Magazine's 500 Greatest Songs of All Time*

When an industrial accident left guitarist Tony Iommi without the tips of two of his fingers, it seemed like death for Black Sabbath. But he fashioned replacements out of pieces of a bottle and developed a playing style that would yield the riff that would define heavy metal forever.

Appears on: Paranoid (Warner Bros.)

(Music appears on page 149)

Kashmir
Led Zeppelin

Written by: John Bonham, Jimmy Page, Robert Plant
Produced by: Page
Released: March '75 on Swan Song
Charts: non-single
»No. 140 *from Rolling Stone® Magazine's 500 Greatest Songs of All Time*

While vacationing in southern Morocco, Plant conjured the lyrics for Led Zeppelin's most ambitious experiment, the centerpiece of 1975's *Physical Graffiti*. As he traveled the desert in northwest Africa, Plant envisioned himself driving straight through to Kashmir. Meanwhile, back in the band's studio in rural England, Page and Bonham began riffing on an Arabic-sounding set of chords that would perfectly match Plant's desert vision. John Paul Jones' string arrangement provided the crowning touch, ratcheting up the song's mystic grandeur to stadium-rock proportion.

Appears on: Physical Graffiti (Atlantic)

(Music appears on page 178)

Knocking on Heaven's Door
Bob Dylan

Written by: Dylan
Produced by: Gordon Carroll
Released: July '73 on Columbia
Charts: 16 weeks; top spot no. 12
»No. 190 *from Rolling Stone® Magazine's 500 Greatest Songs of All Time*

Three years had passed since his last studio album, and Dylan seemed at a loss. So he accepted an invitation to go to Mexico for Sam Peckinpah's *Pat Garrett and Billy the Kid*, for which he shot a bit part and did the soundtrack. For a death scene, Dylan delivered this tale of a dying sheriff, who wants only to lay his "guns in the ground."

Appears on: The Essential Bob Dylan (Sony)

(Music appears on page 184)

Layla
Derek and the Dominos

Written by: Eric Clapton, Jim Gordon
Produced by: Tom Dowd and the Dominos
Released: Nov. '70 on Atco
Charts: 15 weeks; top spot no. 10

»No. 27 *from Rolling Stone® Magazine's 500 Greatest Songs of All Time*

Embroiled in a love triangle with George and Patti Boyd Harrison, Clapton took the title for his greatest song from the Persian love story "Layla and Majnoun." Recorded by Derek and the Dominos – a short-lived ensemble that matched Clapton with members of Delaney and Bonnie's band – "Layla" storms with aching vocals and crosscutting riffs from Clapton and contributing guitarist Duane Allman, then dissolves into a serene, piano-based coda. "It was the heaviest thing going on at the time," Clapton told *Rolling Stone* in 1974. "That's what I wanted to write about most of all."

Appears on: Layla and Other Assorted Love Songs (Polydor)

(Music appears on page 186)

Like a Prayer
Madonna

Written by: Madonna, Patrick Leonard
Produced by: Madonna, Leonard
Released: March '89 on Sire
Charts: 16 weeks; top spot no. 1

»No. 300 *from Rolling Stone® Magazine's 500 Greatest Songs of All Time*

Madonna sang "Like a Prayer" in a voice full of Catholic angst and disco thunder. It was her big personal statement as she turned thirty and closed the book on her first marriage. "I didn't have the censors on me in terms of emotions or music," Madonna said. "I did take a lot more chances with this one, but obviously success gives you the confidence to do those things." The obligatory controversial video featured burning crosses, black lingerie and masturbation in church.

Appears on: Like a Prayer (Warner Bros.)

(Music appears on page 192)

Lola
The Kinks

Written by: Ray Davies
Produced by: Davies
Released: Aug. '70 on Reprise
Charts: 14 weeks; top spot no. 9

»No. 422 *from Rolling Stone® Magazine's 500 Greatest Songs of All Time*

The real Lola? Perhaps transvestite Candy Darling, whom Davies dated. "It was the stubble that gave it away," Ray said.

Appears on: Lola Versus Powerman and the Moneygoround, Part One (Warner Bros.)

(Music appears on page 198)

London Calling
The Clash

Written by: Mick Jones, Joe Strummer
Produced by: Guy Stevens
Released: Jan. '80 on Epic
Charts: did not chart

»No. 15 *from Rolling Stone® Magazine's 500 Greatest Songs of All Time*

Named after the call signal of the BBC's World Service broadcasts, the title alarm of the Clash's third album was an SOS from the heart of darkness. When they recorded the song, the Clash – British punk's most political and uncompromising band – were without management and sinking in debt. Around them, Britain was suffocating in crisis: soaring unemployment, racial conflict, epidemic drug use. "We felt that we were struggling," Joe Strummer said, "about to slip down a slope or something, grasping with our fingernails. And there was no one there to help us."

Strummer and guitarist Mick Jones channeled that trial and worry into a song, produced with hellbent atmosphere by Guy Stevens, that sounded like the Clash marching into battle: Strummer and Jones punching their guitars in metallic unison with Paul Simonon's thumping bass and Topper Headon's rifle-crack drumming. Over that urgency, Strummer howled through a catalog of disasters, real and imagined. The "nuclear error" referred to the March 1979 meltdown of a reactor at Three Mile Island in Pennsylvania. The line "London is drowning/And I live by the river" – Don Letts' video of the Clash shows them playing the song on a boat on the Thames in drenching rain – was based on local folklore. "They say that if the Thames ever flooded, we'd all be underwater," Jones said – except Strummer was living in a high-rise flat at the time, "so he wouldn't have drowned."

Appears on: London Calling (Epic)

(Music appears on page 202)

Losing My Religion
R.E.M.

Written by: Berry, Buck, Mills, Stipe
Produced by: Scott Litt, R.E.M.
Released: March '91 on Warner Bros.
Charts: 21 weeks; top spot no. 4
»**No. 169** *from Rolling Stone® Magazine's 500 Greatest Songs of All Time*

"Losing My Religion" is built around acoustic guitar and mandolin, not exactly a familiar sound on pop radio in the early Nineties – singer Michael Stipe called it a "freak hit." As for the subject matter, it's not religion: "I wanted to write a classic obsession song," he said. "So I did."

Appears on: Out of Time (Warner Bros.)

(Music appears on page 208)

Lust for Life
Iggy Pop

Written by: David Bowie, Pop
Produced by: Bowie
Released: Sept. '77 on RCA
Charts: did not chart
»**No. 147** *from Rolling Stone® Magazine's 500 Greatest Songs of All Time*

With its enormous kaboom and Pop's sneering, free-associative lyrics (the line about "hypnotizing chickens" is a reference to William S. Burroughs' *The Ticket That Exploded*), "Lust for Life" is half a kiss-off to drugged-out hedonism, half a French kiss to it. Nineteen years after the song first appeared, it was used in the 1996 movie *Trainspotting*, paving the way for cleaned-up versions to be used in TV ads for cars and cruise lines. And what about the line "Of course I've had it in the ear before"? "That's a common expression in the Midwest," Pop said. "To give it to him right in the ear means to fuck somebody over."

Appears on: Lust for Life (Virgin)

(Music appears on page 214)

Maggie May
Rod Stewart

Written by: Stewart, Martin Quittenton
Produced by: Stewart
Released: June '71 on Mercury
Charts: 17 weeks; top spot no. 1
»**No. 130** *from Rolling Stone® Magazine's 500 Greatest Songs of All Time*

Stewart plays a schoolboy in love with an older temptress in "Maggie May," trying desperately to subdue his hormones with common sense. The song was a last-minute addition to the LP *Every Picture Tells a Story* and was initially the B side of "Reason to Believe." Stewart has joked that if a DJ hadn't flipped the single over, he'd have gone back to his old job: digging graves. But the song's rustic country mandolin and acoustic guitars – and Mickey Waller's simple but relentless drum-bashing – were undeniable.

Appears on: Every Picture Tells a Story (Mercury/Universal)

(Music appears on page 220)

Moondance
Van Morrison

Written by: Morrison
Produced by: Morrison
Released: Feb. '70 on Warner Bros.
Charts: 4 weeks; top spot no. 92
»**No. 226** *from Rolling Stone® Magazine's 500 Greatest Songs of All Time*

The title song of Morrison's first self-produced album started "as a saxophone solo," he said. "I used to play this sax number over and over, anytime I picked up my horn." He played the sax solo on this recording, which combined the bucolic charm of his life in Woodstock, New York ("the cover of October skies"), with his love of the sophisticated jazz and R&B of Mose Allison and Ray Charles.

Appears on: Moondance (Warner Bros.)

(Music appears on page 205)

No Woman, No Cry
Bob Marley and the Wailers

Written by: Vincent Ford, Marley
Produced by: Chris Blackwell, Marley and the Wailers
Released: May '75 on Island
Charts: did not chart
»**No. 37** *from Rolling Stone® Magazine's 500 Greatest Songs of All Time*

The "government yard in Trench Town" refers to the Jamaican public-housing project where Marley lived in the late Fifties. Marley gave a songwriting credit on "No Woman, No Cry" to childhood friend Vincent "Tata" Ford in order to help keep Ford's Kingston soup kitchen running.

Appears on: Natty Dread (Island)

(Music appears on page 224)

Paradise City
Guns n' Roses

Written by: Axl Rose, Duff McKagan, Izzy Stradlin, Slash, Steven Adler
Produced by: Mike Clink
Released: Aug. '87 on Geffen
Charts: 17 weeks; top spot no. 5
»**No. 453** *from Rolling Stone® Magazine's 500 Greatest Songs of All Time*

"Paradise City" elevated Axl and Slash to rock's Mount Olympus. For nearly seven minutes, they expound on the joys of green grass, pretty girls and toxic chemicals. In a typically tasteful Gn'R move, the video features footage of the band's 1988 gig at Castle Donington in the U.K. – where two fans were crushed to death.

Appears on: Appetite for Destruction

(Music appears on page 227)

Paranoid
Black Sabbath

Written by: Geezer Butler, Tony Iommi, Ozzy Osbourne, William Ward
Produced by: Rodger Bain
Released: Nov.'70 on Warner Bros.
Charts: 8 weeks; top spot no. 61

»No. 250 *from Rolling Stone® Magazine's 500 Greatest Songs of All Time*

After Sabbath's first U.S. tour, guitarist Tony Iommi hunkered down at Regent Studios in London, trying to write one more song for the group's second album. "I started fiddling about on the guitar and came up with this riff," he said. "When the others came back [from lunch], we recorded it on the spot." "Paranoid," a two-minute blast of protopunk, became Sabbath's biggest single. It is also proof of the short distance between heavy metal and the Ramones.

Appears on: Paranoid (Castle)

(Music appears on page 236)

Paranoid Android
Radiohead

Written by: Thom Yorke
Produced by: Nigel Godrich, Radiohead
Released: May '97 on Capitol
Charts: did not chart

»No. 256 *from Rolling Stone® Magazine's 500 Greatest Songs of All Time*

"'Paranoid Android' is about the dullest fucking people on earth," said singer Yorke, referring to lyrics such as "Squealing Gucci little piggy," about a creepy coked-out woman he once spied at an L.A. bar. The sound was just as unnerving: a shape-shifting, three-part prog-rock suite. Spooky fact: It was recorded in actress Jane Seymour's fifteenth-century mansion, a house that Yorke was convinced was haunted.

Appears on: OK Computer (Capitol)

(Music appears on page 240)

(What's So Funny 'Bout) Peace Love and Understanding?
Elvis Costello and the Attractions

Written by: Nick Lowe
Produced by: Lowe
Released: Jan.'79 on Columbia
Charts: non-single

»No. 284 *from Rolling Stone® Magazine's 500 Greatest Songs of All Time*

"What's So Funny" was written by Lowe, Costello's pal and producer. The original, by Lowe's country-rock band Brinsley Schwartz, was mellow and cute, but Costello snarls the song intensely enough to make the title question seem brand-new, with thundering drums and droning piano. It's like Abba playing punk rock.

Appears on: Armed Forces (Rhino)

(Music appears on page 246)

Personality Crisis
New York Dolls

Written by: David Johansen, Johnny Thunders
Produced by: Todd Rundgren
Released: Aug.'73 on Mercury
Charts: did not chart

»No. 267 *from Rolling Stone® Magazine's 500 Greatest Songs of All Time*

No song better captured the New York Dolls' glammed-out R&B than "Personality Crisis," the opening track on the group's debut album. Produced by Rundgren during an eight-day session, "Personality Crisis" was the trashy sound of an identity meltdown. Soon after, the Dolls fell victim to one themselves and dissolved amid a haze of drugs.

Appears on: New York Dolls (Mercury)

(Music appears on page 248)

Radio Free Europe
R.E.M.

Written by: Berry, Buck, Mills, Stipe
Produced by: Mitch Easter, Don Dixon
Released: July '83 on I.R.S.
Charts: 5 weeks; top spot no. 78

»No. 379 *from Rolling Stone® Magazine's 500 Greatest Songs of All Time*

"We hated it," said Peter Buck of the sound on the first version of "Europe," on indie label Hib-Tone. "It was mastered by a deaf man, apparently." The band rerecorded it for *Murmur*.

Appears on: Murmur (A&M)

(Music appears on page 254)

(Don't Fear) the Reaper
Blue Öyster Cult

Written by: Donald Roeser
Produced by: Murray Krugman, Sandy Pearlman, David Lucas
Released: July '76 on Columbia
Charts: 14 weeks; top spot no. 12
»No. 397 *from Rolling Stone® Magazine's 500 Greatest Songs of All Time*

This Long Island metal band's death trip was picked by *Rolling Stone* critics as the best rock single of 1976. With its ghostly guitars and cowbell, "Reaper" has added chills to horror flicks from *Halloween* to *The Stand*. Bonus points for the crackpot theology about how "40,000 men and women every day" join Romeo and Juliet in eternity.

Appears on: Agents of Fortune (Columbia)

(Music appears on page 258)

Respect
Aretha Franklin

Written by: Otis Redding
Produced by: Jerry Wexler
Released: April '67 on Atlantic
Charts: 12 weeks; top spot no. 1
»No. 5 *from Rolling Stone® Magazine's 500 Greatest Songs of All Time*

Otis Redding wrote "Respect" and recorded it first, for the Volt label in 1965. But Aretha Franklin took possession of the song for all time with her definitive cover, made at Atlantic's New York studio on Valentine's Day 1967. "Respect" was her first Number One hit and the single that established her as the Queen of Soul. In Redding's reading, a brawny march powered by Booker T. and the MG's and the Memphis Horns, he called for equal favor with volcanic force. Franklin wasn't asking for anything. She sang from higher ground: a woman calling an end to the exhaustion and sacrifice of a raw deal with scorching sexual authority. In short, if you want some, you will earn it.

"For Otis, *respect* had the traditional connotation, the more abstract meaning of esteem," Franklin's producer, Jerry Wexler, said in his autobiography, *Rhythm and the Blues: A Life in American Music.* "The fervor in Aretha's voice demanded that respect; and more respect also involved sexual attention of the highest order. What else would 'sock it to me' mean?"

He was referring to the knockout sound of Franklin's backup singers – her sisters Carolyn and Erma – chanting "Sock it to me" at high speed, which Aretha and Carolyn cooked up for the session. The late Tom Dowd, who engineered the date, credited Carolyn with the saucy breakdown in which Aretha spelled out the title: "I fell off my chair when I heard that!" And since Redding's version had no bridge, Wexler had the studio band – the crew from Muscle Shoals, Alabama, that had cut Franklin's Atlantic debut, "I Never Loved a Man (the Way I Love You)," a month before – play the chord changes from Sam and Dave's "When Something Is Wrong With My Baby" under King Curtis' tenor-sax solo.

There is no mistaking the passion inside the discipline of Franklin's delivery; she was surely drawing on her own tumultuous marriage at the time for inspiration. "If she didn't live it," Wexler said, "she couldn't give it." But, he added, "Aretha would never play the part of the scorned woman…. Her middle name was Respect."

Appears on: I Never Loved a Man the Way I Love You (Atlantic)

(Music appears on page 268)

Sheena Is a Punk Rocker
Ramones

Written by: Ramones
Produced by: Tony Bongiovi, T. Erdelyi
Released: May '77 on Sire
Charts: 13 weeks; top spot no. 81
»No. 457 *from Rolling Stone® Magazine's 500 Greatest Songs of All Time*

This mash note to surfing, punk girls and New York was actually cut twice: first as a single that was rushed to radio and became one of the Ramones' few, modest hits, then in a slightly souped-up version for the band's third album, *Rocket to Russia*. "I combined Sheena, Queen of the Jungle with the primalness of punk rock," said singer Joey Ramone. "It was funny, because all the girls in New York seemed to change their names to Sheena after that."

Appears on: Rocket to Russia (Rhino)

(Music appears on page 272)

Should I Stay or Should I Go
The Clash

Written by: The Clash
Produced by: Glyn Johns
Released: May '82 on Epic
Charts: 13 weeks; top spot no. 45
»No. 228 *from Rolling Stone® Magazine's 500 Greatest Songs of All Time*

"My main influences," Mick Jones said "are Mott the Hoople, the Kinks and the Stones" – which explains the choppy riff here. The hellbent chorus hints at the end: At the time, "none of us were really talking to each other," said Paul Simonon. The original four were soon no more.

Appears on: Combat Rock (Sony)

(Music appears on page 276)

Spirit in the Sky
Norman Greenbaum

Written by: Greenbaum
Produced by: Erik Jacobsen
Released: Feb. '70 on Reprise
Charts: 15 weeks; top spot no. 3

»No. 333 *from Rolling Stone® Magazine's 500 Greatest Songs of All Time*

Greenbaum's "Spirit in the Sky" was unusual at the time for its crunchy guitar sound, which came when a friend built a small fuzz box right into the body of Greenbaum's Fender Telecaster, as well as for its subject matter: Jesus and death. "I'm just some Jewish musician who really dug gospel music," Greenbaum said. "I decided there was a larger Jesus gospel market out there than a Jehovah one."

Appears on: Spirit in the Sky (Varese)

(Music appears on page 280)

Stairway to Heaven
Led Zeppelin

Written by: Jimmy Page, Robert Plant
Produced by: Page
Released: Nov. '71 on Atlantic
Charts: non-single

»No. 31 *from Rolling Stone® Magazine's 500 Greatest Songs of All Time*

All epic anthems must measure themselves against "Stairway to Heaven," the cornerstone of *Led Zeppelin IV.* Building from an acoustic intro that sounds positively Elizabethan, thanks to John Paul Jones' recorder solo and Plant's fanciful lyrics, it morphs into a Page solo that storms heaven's gate. Page said the song "crystallized the essence of the band. It had everything there and showed the band at its best.... as a band, as a unit.... It was a milestone for us. Every musician wants to do something of lasting quality, something which will hold up for a long time, and I guess we did it with 'Stairway.'"

Appears on: Led Zeppelin IV (Atlantic)

(Music appears on page 284)

Stayin' Alive
Bee Gees

Written by: Robin Gibb, Barry Gibb, Maurice Gibb
Produced by: Barry Gibb, Robin Gibb, Maurice Gibb, Karl Richardson, Albhy Galuten
Released: Nov. '77 on RSO
Charts: 27 weeks; top spot no. 1

»No. 189 *from Rolling Stone® Magazine's 500 Greatest Songs of All Time*

This disco classic was written after Robert Stigwood asked the Bee Gees for music for a film he was producing based on a *New York* magazine account of the Brooklyn club scene.

Appears on: Saturday Night Fever (Polydor)

(Music appears on page 265)

Sweet Child O' Mine
Guns n' Roses

Written by: Guns n' Roses
Produced by: Mike Clink
Released: Aug. '87 on Geffen
Charts: 24 weeks; top spot no. 1

»No. 196 *from Rolling Stone® Magazine's 500 Greatest Songs of All Time*

In the midst of an album full of songs about cheap drugs and cheaper sex came Axl Rose's love letter to his girlfriend, Erin Everly (daughter of Don Everly). Slash has said he was just "fucking around with the intro riff, making a joke"; neither he nor the rest of the band thought much of it, but Rose knew better. Rose and Erin Everly were later married – for all of one month.

Appears on: Appetite for Destruction (Geffen)

(Music appears on page 292)

Tangled Up in Blue
Bob Dylan

Written by: Dylan
Produced by: Dylan
Released: Jan. '75 on Columbia
Charts: 7 weeks; top spot no. 31

»No. 68 *from Rolling Stone® Magazine's 500 Greatest Songs of All Time*

When Dylan introduced "Tangled Up in Blue" onstage in 1978, he described it as a song that took him "ten years to live and two years to write." It's still one of his most frequently performed live staples. It was the six-minute opener from *Blood on the Tracks*, written as his first marriage was falling apart. Dylan takes inspiration from classic country singers such as Hank Williams and Lefty Frizzell, in a tale of a drifting heart on the road through the Sixties and Seventies. Dylan kept revising the song heavily through the years; on his 1984 *Real Live*, he plays with the chords and lyrics to tell a whole new story.

Appears on: Blood on the Tracks (Columbia)

(Music appears on page 300)

Thank You (Falettinme Be Mice Elf Agin)
Sly and the Family Stone

Written by: Sylvester Stewart
Produced by: Stewart
Released: Jan. '70 on Epic
Charts: 13 weeks; top spot no. 1

»No. 402 *from Rolling Stone® Magazine's 500 Greatest Songs of All Time*

"Thank you" rode on the finger-popping bass of Larry Graham, who came up with the technique in a duo with his organist mother. "I started to thump the strings with my thumb," he said, "to make up for not having a drummer."

Appears on: Anthology (Epic)

(Music appears on page 302)

Thunder Road
Bruce Springsteen

Written by: Springsteen
Produced by: Springsteen, Jon Landau, Mike Appel
Released: Aug. '75 on Columbia
Charts: non-single

»No. 86 *from Rolling Stone® Magazine's 500 Greatest Songs of All Time*

"We decided to make a guitar album, but then I wrote all the songs on piano," Springsteen said of his third album, *Born to Run.* "Thunder Road," its opening track, is a cinematic tale of redemption with a title borrowed from a 1958 hillbilly noir starring Robert Mitchum as a bootlegger with a car that can't be beat. These days, with Springsteen in his midfifties, he marvels that he wrote the line "You're scared, and you're thinking that maybe we ain't that young any more" when he was all of twenty-four years old.

Appears on: Born to Run (Columbia)

(Music appears on page 304)

Walk on the Wild Side
Lou Reed

Written by: Reed
Produced by: David Bowie, Mick Ronson, Reed
Released: Dec. '72 on RCA
Charts: 14 weeks; top spot no. 16

»No. 221 *from Rolling Stone® Magazine's 500 Greatest Songs of All Time*

After Reed left the Velvet Underground in 1970, he was asked to write songs for a musical based on Nelson Algren's novel *A Walk on the Wild Side.* The show was never mounted, but Reed kept the title and applied it to characters he knew from Andy Warhol's Factory. "I always thought it would be kinda fun to introduce people you see at parties but don't dare approach," said Reed.

Appears on: Transformer (RCA)

(Music appears on page 297)

Welcome to the Jungle
Guns n' Roses

Written by: Guns n' Roses
Produced by: Mike Clink
Released: Aug. '87 on Geffen
Charts: 17 weeks; top spot no. 7

»No. 467 *from Rolling Stone® Magazine's 500 Greatest Songs of All Time*

In which Gn'R beckoned listeners into their sordid Hollywood milieu. Guns' five-year reign as the globe's biggest rock band begins here.

Appears on: Appetite for Destruction (Geffen)

(Music appears on page 310)

What's Going On
Marvin Gaye

Written by: Gaye, Renaldo Benson, Al Cleveland
Produced by: Gaye
Released: Feb. '71 on Tamla
Charts: 13 weeks; top spot no. 2

》No. 4 *from Rolling Stone® Magazine's 500 Greatest Songs of All Time*

"What's Going On" is an exquisite plea for peace on earth, sung by a man at the height of crisis. In 1970, Marvin Gaye was Motown's top male vocal star, yet he was frustrated by the assembly-line role he played on his own hits. Devastated by the loss of duet partner Tammi Terrell, who died that March after a three-year battle with a brain tumor, Gaye was also trapped in a turbulent marriage to Anna Gordy, Motown boss Berry Gordy's sister. Gaye was tormented, too, by his relationship with his puritanical father, Marvin Sr. "If I was arguing for peace," Gaye told biographer David Ritz, "I knew I'd have to find peace in my heart."

Not long after Terrell's passing, Renaldo Benson of the Four Tops presented Gaye with a song he had written with Motown staffer Al Cleveland. Benson later claimed that he gave Gaye a co-writing credit as an inducement to sing and produce the track. But Gaye made the song his own: directly overseeing the liquid beauty of David Van DePitte's arrangement (although Gaye could not read or write music) and investing the topical references to war and racial strife with private anguish. Motown session crew the Funk Brothers cut the stunning, jazz-inflected rhythm track, which was unlike anything in the label's Sixties hit parade (Gaye played cardboard-box percussion). Then Gaye invoked his own family in moving prayer: singing to his younger brother Frankie, a Vietnam veteran ("Brother, brother, brother/There's far too many of you dying"), and appealing for calm closer to home ("Father, father, father/We don't need to escalate").

Initially rejected as uncommercial, "What's Going On" (with background vocals by two players from the Detroit Lions) was Gaye's finest studio achievement, a timeless gift of healing. But for Gaye, the peace he craved never came: On April 1st, 1984, he died in a family dispute – shot by his father.

Appears on: What's Going On (Tamla)

(Music appears on page 317)

Whipping Post
The Allman Brothers Band

Written by: Gregg Allman
Produced by: Tom Dowd
Released: Nov. '69 on Capricorn
Charts: non-single

》No. 383 *from Rolling Stone® Magazine's 500 Greatest Songs of All Time*

This enduring anthem was written on an ironing board in a darkened Florida bedroom by Allman. Leaping off with a rumbling Berry Oakley bass line, rife with tormented blues-ballad imagery and punctuated by Duane Allman's knifelike guitar incisions, the song is best appreciated in the twenty-three-minute incarnation on *At Fillmore East*.

Appears on: At Fillmore East (Mercury)

(Music appears on page 320)

Whole Lotta Love
Led Zeppelin

Written by: Willie Dixon, Led Zeppelin
Produced by: Jimmy Page
Released: Oct. '69 on Atlantic
Charts: 15 weeks; top spot no. 4

》No. 75 *from Rolling Stone® Magazine's 500 Greatest Songs of All Time*

When Page recruited his new band, Led Zeppelin, the four musicians got their sound together by jamming on the blues standards they loved, stretching them out into psychedelic orgies. "Whole Lotta Love" was their tribute to Chicago blues songwriter Willie Dixon. It was based on his "You Need Love," a single Muddy Waters cut in 1962, though Plant also threw in quotes from songs Dixon wrote for Howlin' Wolf: "Shake for Me" and "Back Door Man." Avowed Dixon fans, the band also covered "You Shook Me," "I Can't Quit You Baby" and "Bring It On Home" on its first two albums – but never sorted out the copyright issues until 1985, when Dixon brought legal action and got his rightful share of the credit for "Whole Lotta Love." "Page's riff was Page's riff," Plant said. "I just thought, 'Well, what am I going to sing?' That was it, a nick. Now happily paid for." Said Page, "Usually my riffs are pretty damn original. What can I say?"

Appears on: Led Zeppelin II (Atlantic)

(Music appears on page 332)

Wild Horses
The Rolling Stones

Written by: Mick Jagger, Keith Richards
Produced by: Jimmy Miller
Released: April '71 on Rolling Stones
Charts: 8 weeks; top spot no. 28

»No. 334 *from Rolling Stone® Magazine's 500 Greatest Songs of All Time*

Richards wrote this acoustic ballad about leaving his wife Anita and young son Marlon as the Stones prepared for their first American tour in three years. Stones sidekick Ian Stewart refused to play the minor chords required, so Memphis musical maverick Jim Dickinson filled in on upright piano at the Muscle Shoals, Alabama, recording session for *Sticky Fingers*.

Appears on: Sticky Fingers (Virgin)

(Music appears on page 336)

Wish You Were Here
Pink Floyd

Written by: David Gilmour, Roger Waters
Produced by: Pink Floyd
Released: Sept. '75 on Columbia
Charts: non-single

»No. 316 *from Rolling Stone® Magazine's 500 Greatest Songs of All Time*

While Pink Floyd were recording this elegy for burned-out ex-frontman Syd Barrett, he mysteriously appeared in the studio in such bad shape nobody recognized him. "He stood up and said, 'Right, when do I put my guitar on?'" keyboardist Rick Wright recalled. "And of course, he didn't have a guitar with him. And we said, 'Sorry, Syd, the guitar's all done.'"

Appears on: Wish You Were Here (Capitol)

(Music appears on page 340)

You Can't Always Get What You Want
The Rolling Stones

Written by: Mick Jagger, Keith Richards
Produced by: Jimmy Miller
Released: July '69 on London
Charts: 8 weeks; top spot no. 42

»No. 100 *from Rolling Stone® Magazine's 500 Greatest Songs of All Time*

After a November 1968 recording session at Olympic Studio in London, Al Kooper told Jagger he wanted to take a crack at some horn charts for the song they had just finished recording. Kooper got his wish, but only his French horn made the final mix, providing "You Can't Always Get What You Want" with its signature intro. Kooper copped the song's piano groove from an Etta James record, and producer Miller – "Mr. Jimmy" in the Jagger lyric – subbed on the trap kit for the usually unerring Charlie Watts when the Stones drummer had difficulty mastering the tricky groove. Phil Spector accomplice Jack Nitzsche provided the crowning touch in March 1969, orchestrating the London Bach Choir into a towering backing chorus. The song would provide a grandiose finale for a landmark album.

Appears on: Let It Bleed (ABKCO)

(Music appears on page 325)

ALISON

Words and Music by
ELVIS COSTELLO

Alison - 4 - 1

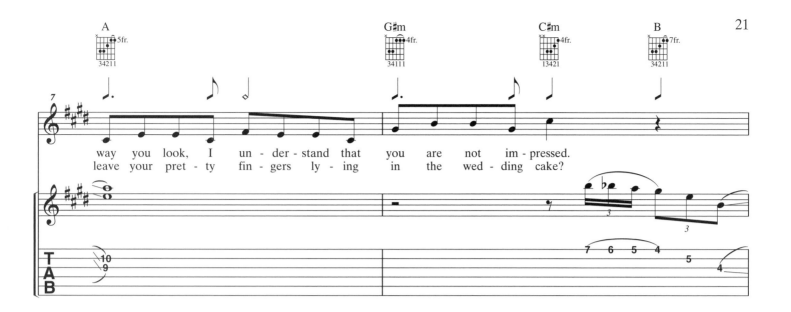

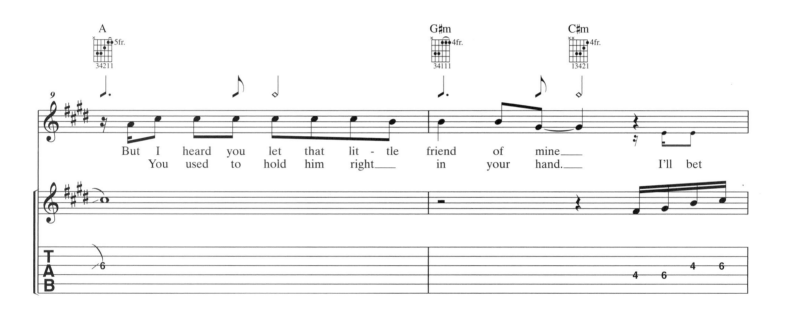

Chorus:

Al - i - son,_____ I know_____ this world_____ is kill -

- ing you. Oh,_____ Al - i - son,_____

my aim_____ is true._____

My aim_____ is true._____

Repeat ad lib. and fade

ANOTHER BRICK IN THE WALL (PART 2)

Moderately ♩ = 104

Words and Music by
ROGER WATERS

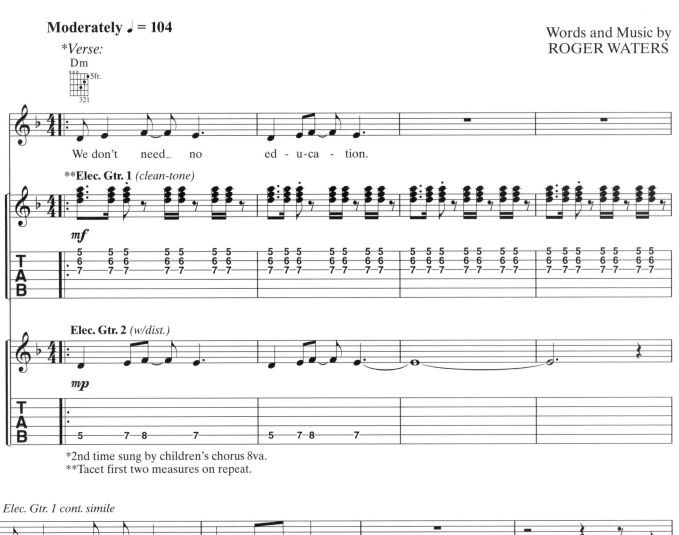

*2nd time sung by children's chorus 8va.
**Tacet first two measures on repeat.

Another Brick in the Wall (Part 2) - 5 - 1

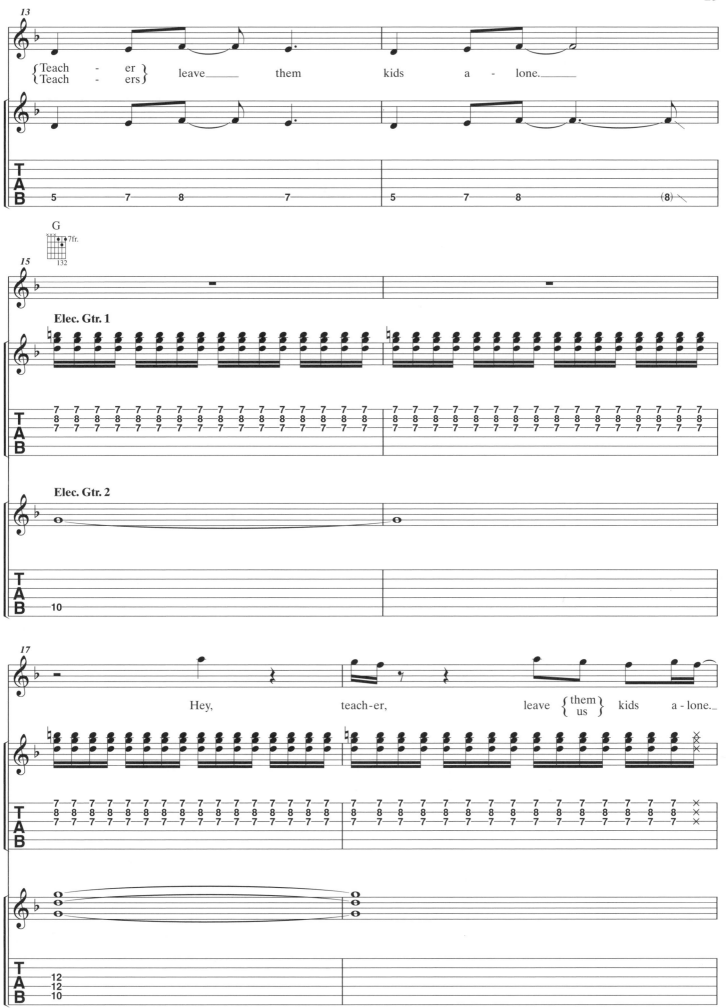

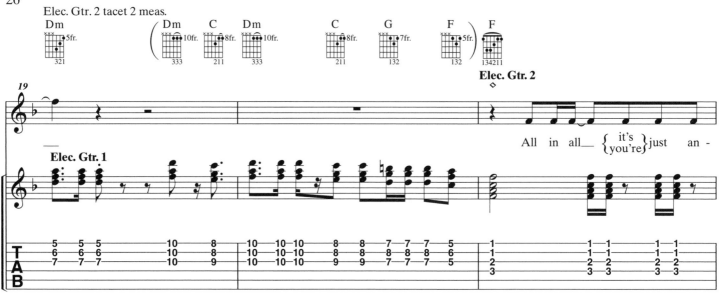

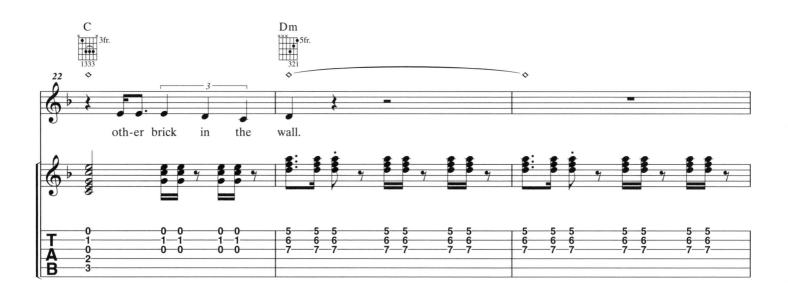

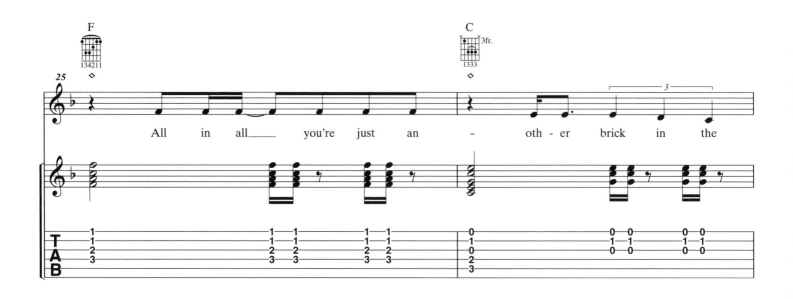

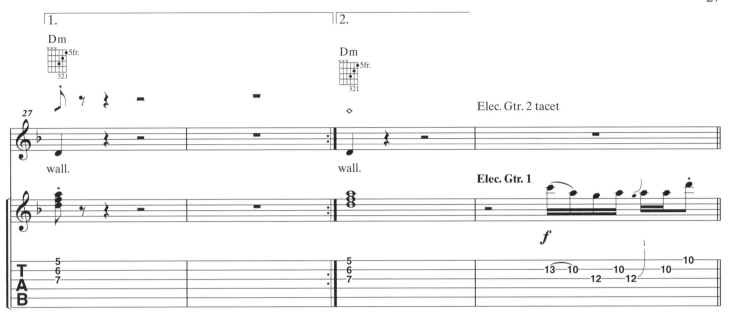

Guitar Solo:

* Dm

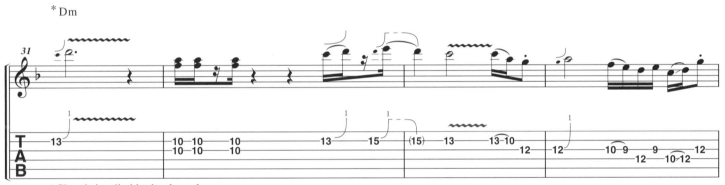

*Chords implied by keyboards.

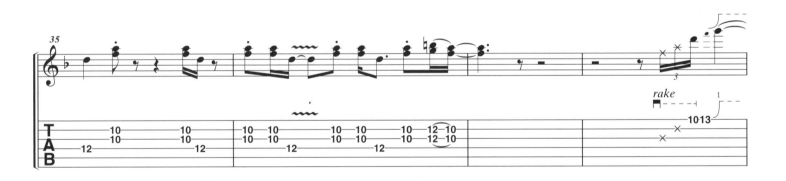

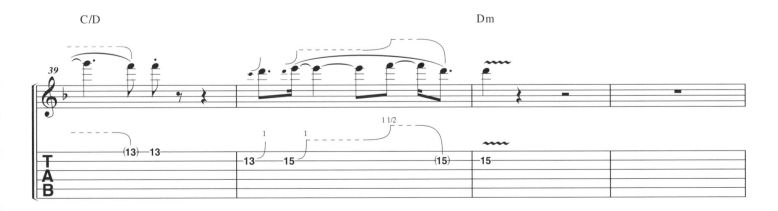

Outro: *Repeat ad lib. and fade*

BACK IN BLACK

Words and Music by
ANGUS YOUNG, MALCOLM YOUNG
and BRIAN JOHNSON

1. Back in black, I hit the sack, I've been too long, I'm glad to be back, yes, I
2. *See additional lyrics*

*Vocal sounds 8va on recording.

am. Let loose from the noose that's kept me hangin' a-bout. I've been

liv-in' like a star 'cause it's get-tin' me high, for-get the hearse 'cause I'll nev-er die. I got

Back in Black - 7 - 1

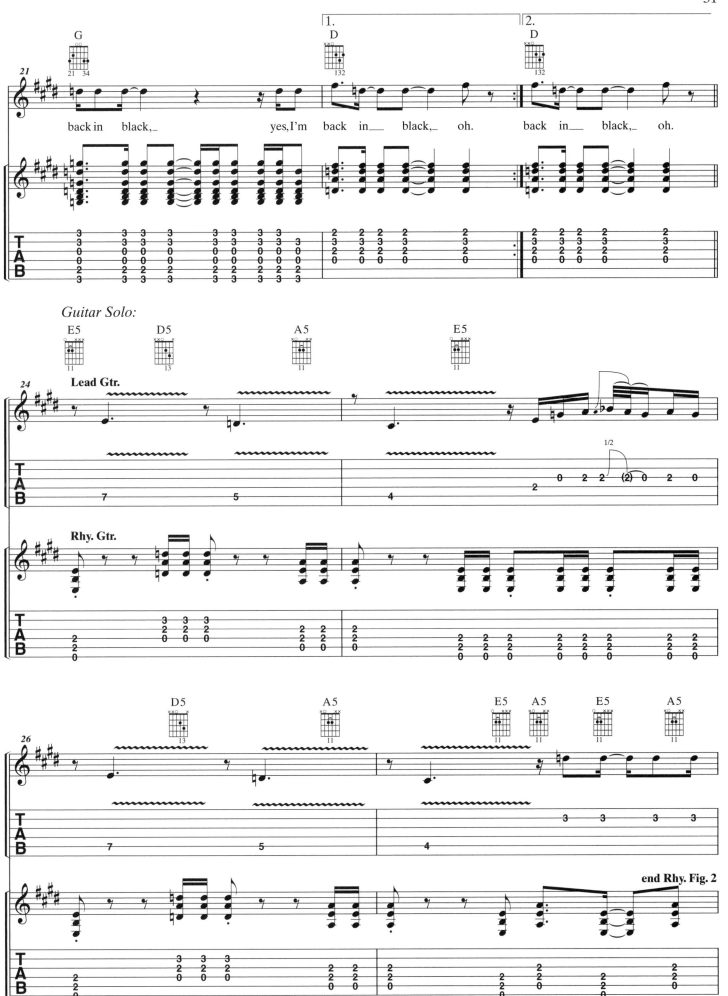

back in black,_   yes, I'm back in_ black,_ oh.   back in_ black,_ oh.

Guitar Solo:

end Rhy. Fig. 2

Outro:
w/Rhy. Fig. 2 *(Rhy. Gtr.)*

Repeat and fade

Lead Gtr. w/ad lib. gtr. fills (use Guitar Solo as a model for improv.)

Verse 2:
Back in the band, I drive a Cadillac,
Number one with a bullet, I'm a power pack.
Yes, I am in a band with a gang,
They got to catch me if they want me to hang.
'Cause I'm back on the track and I'm beatin' the flack,
Nobody's gonna get me on another rap.
So look at me now, I'm just a-makin' my pay.
Don't try to push your luck, just get outta my way.
'Cause I'm back…
(To Chorus:)

BAD MOON RISING

To match record key, tune down one whole step

Words and Music by
J.C. FOGERTY

Bad Moon Rising - 3 - 1

BEAT IT

To match record key, tune down 1/2 step

Written and Composed by
MICHAEL JACKSON

Beat It - 7 - 1

Verse:

1. They told him don't you ev-er come a-round here. Don't wan-na see your face, you bet-ter
2. They're out to get you, bet-ter leave while you can. Don't wan-na be a boy, you wan-na

dis-ap-pear. The fi-re's in their eyes and their words are real-ly clear. So
be a man. You wan-na stay a-live, bet-ter do what you can. So

beat it, just beat it.
beat it, just beat it.

Elec. Gtr. 1

Cont. rhy. simile

You bet-ter run, you bet-ter do what you can. Don't wan-na see no blood, don't be a
You have to show them that you're real-ly not scared. You're play-in' with your life, this ain't no

ma-cho man. You wan-na be tough, bet-ter do what you can. So
truth or dare. They'll kick you, then they beat you, then they'll tell you it's fair. So

Beat It - 7 - 2

beat it, beat it, beat it, beat it. No___ one wants to be de - feat - ed. Show__

___ 'em how funk-y, strong__ is your fight. It___ does-n't mat-ter, who's__wrong or right. Just

w/Rhy. Fig. 2 *(Elec. Gtr. 1) 7 times*

beat it, beat it, beat it. Beat it, beat it.

Rhy. Fig. 2

P.M.

Beat it, beat it. Beat it, beat it.

w/Rhy. Fig. 3 *(Elec. Gtr. 2)* 3 times, simile

43

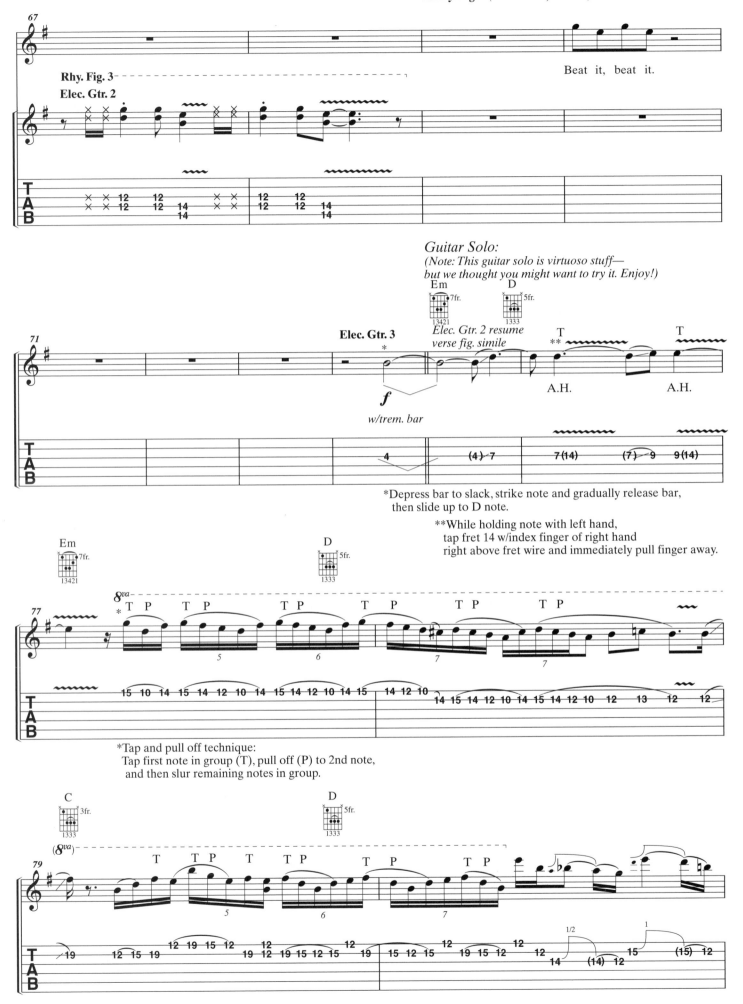

Beat it, beat it.

Guitar Solo:
(Note: This guitar solo is virtuoso stuff—
but we thought you might want to try it. Enjoy!)

*Depress bar to slack, strike note and gradually release bar,
then slide up to D note.

**While holding note with left hand,
tap fret 14 w/index finger of right hand
right above fret wire and immediately pull finger away.

*Tap and pull off technique:
Tap first note in group (T), pull off (P) to 2nd note,
and then slur remaining notes in group.

Beat It - 7 - 5

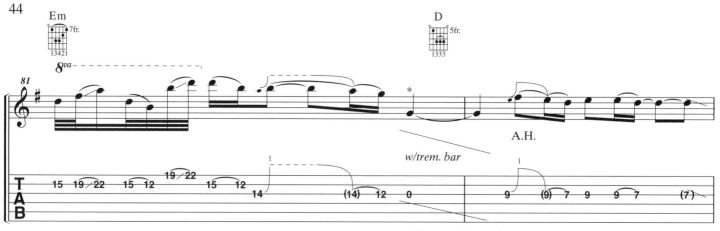

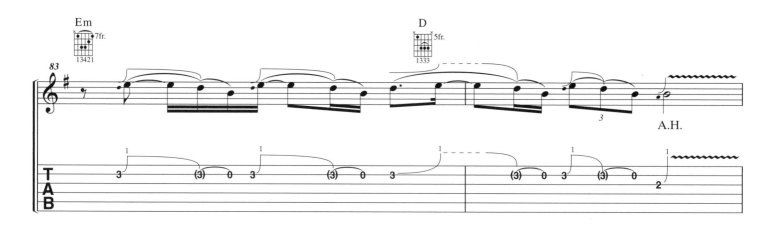

*Depress bar to slack.

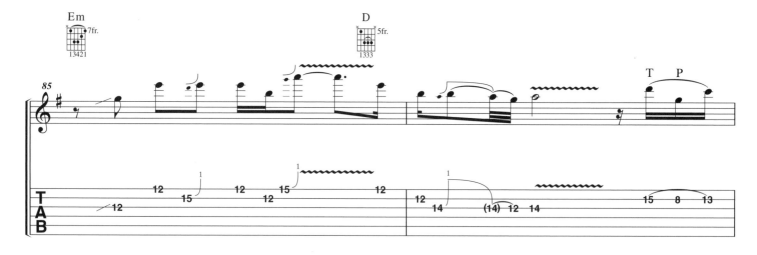

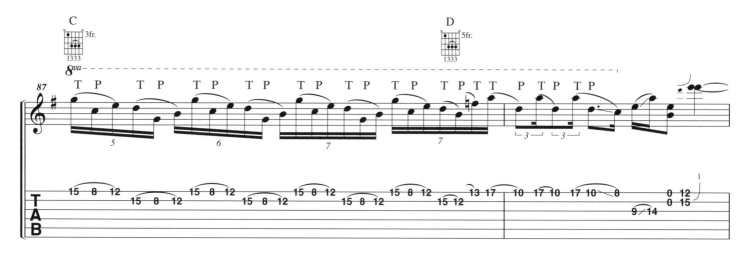

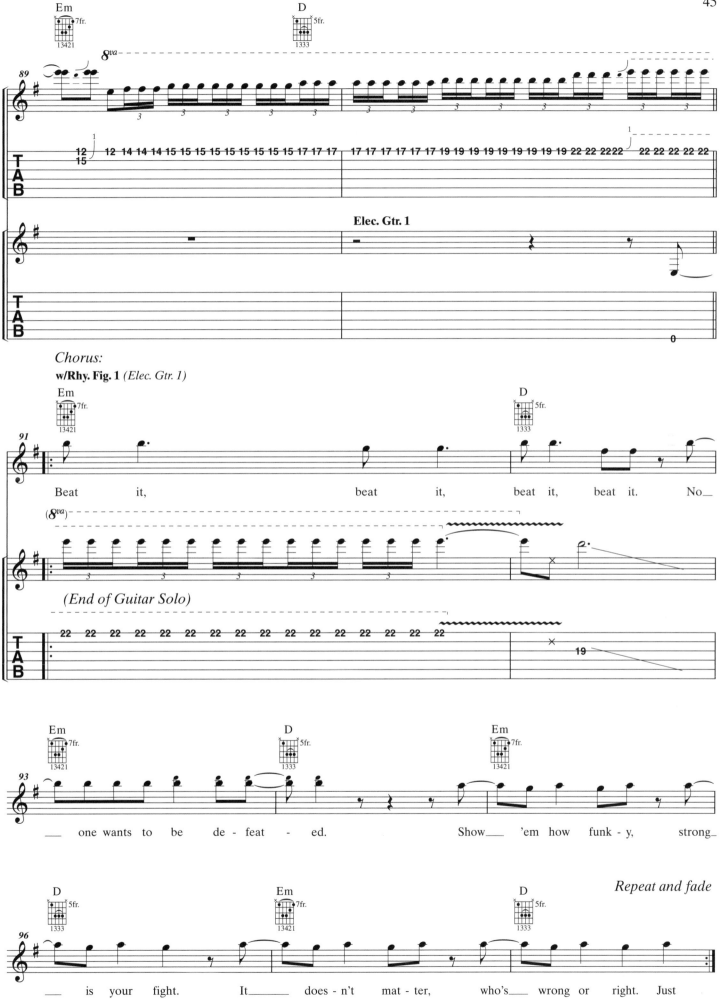

BILLIE JEAN

Words and Music by
MICHAEL JACKSON

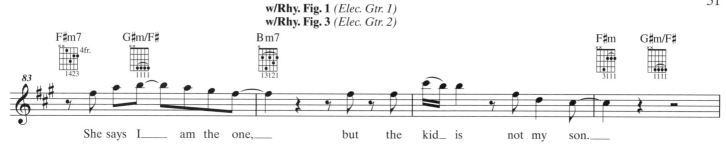

Outro:

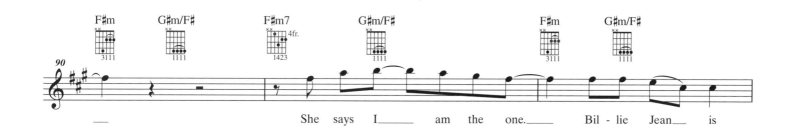

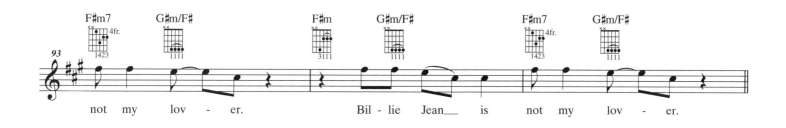

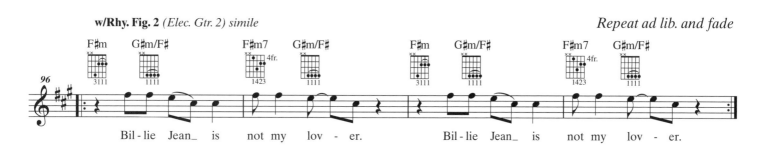

BITTER SWEET SYMPHONY

Words and Music by
MICK JAGGER, KEITH RICHARDS
and RICHARD ASHCROFT

Bitter Sweet Symphony - 3 - 1

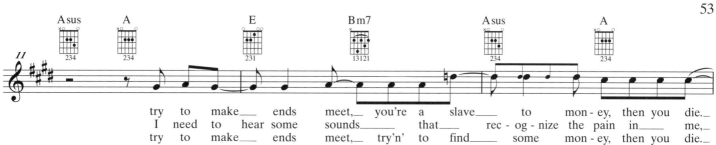

try to make___ ends meet,___ you're a slave___ to mon-ey, then you die.___
I need to hear some sounds___ that___ rec - og - nize the pain in___ me,___
try to make___ ends meet,___ try'n' to find___ some mon-ey, then you die.___

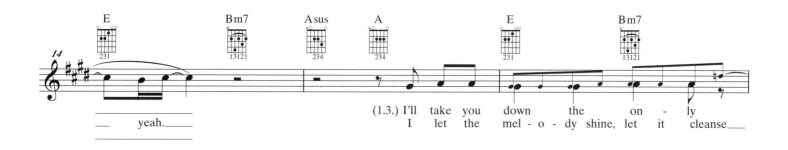

___ yeah.___
___ yeah.___
(1.3.) I'll take you down the on - ly
I let the mel - o - dy shine, let it cleanse___

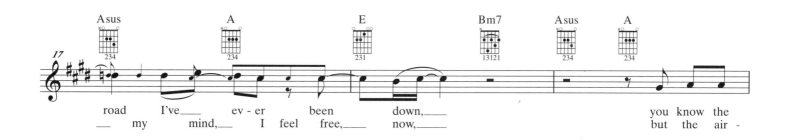

road I've___ ev - er been down,___ you know the
___ my mind,___ I feel free,___ now,___ but the air -

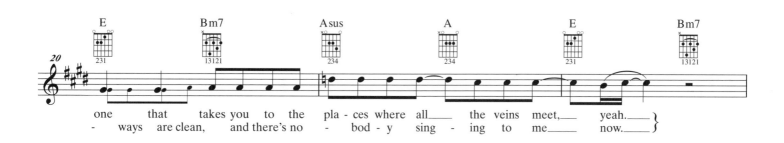

one that takes you to the pla - ces where all___ the veins meet,___ yeah.___}
- ways are clean, and there's no - bod - y sing - ing to me___ now.___}

Elec. Gtr. tacet

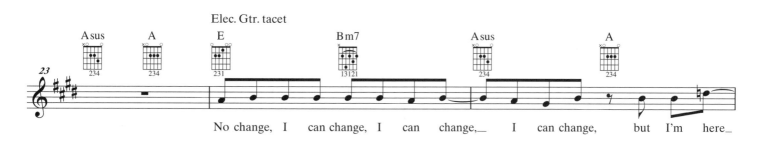

No change, I can change, I can change,___ I can change, but I'm here___

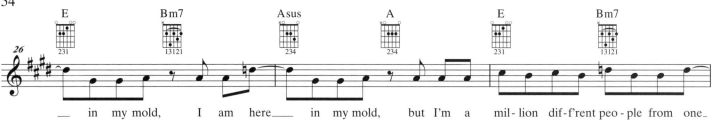

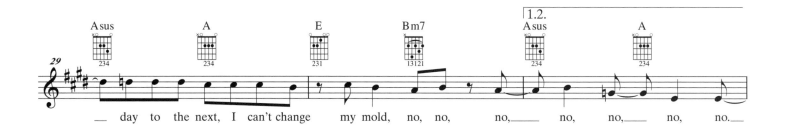

_ in my mold, I am here____ in my mold, but I'm a mil-lion dif-f'rent peo-ple from one_

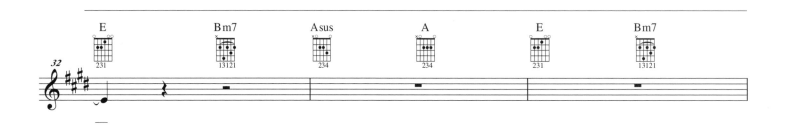

_ day to the next, I can't change my mold, no, no, no,____ no, no,____ no, no.____

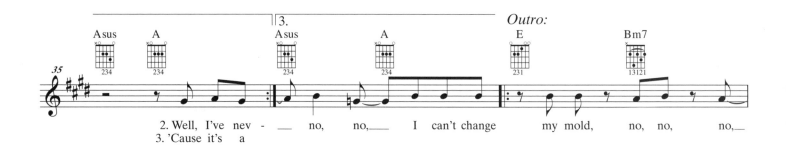

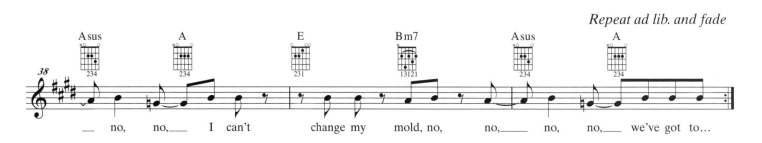

2. Well, I've nev - __ no, no,____ I can't change my mold, no, no, no,____
3. 'Cause it's a

Outro:

Repeat ad lib. and fade

_ no, no,____ I can't change my mold, no, no,____ no, no,____ we've got to...

Bitter Sweet Symphony - 3 - 3

BLACK DOG

Words and Music by
JIMMY PAGE, ROBERT PLANT
and JOHN PAUL JONES

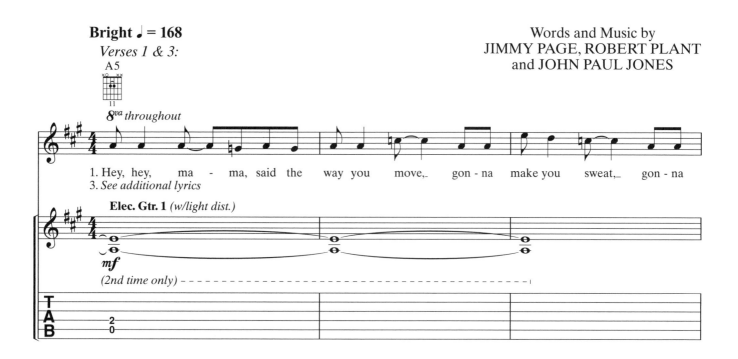

make you   sting.

Hey, hey,   ba - by, when you walk that   way,_ watch your hon-ey   drip,_ can't keep a - way.___

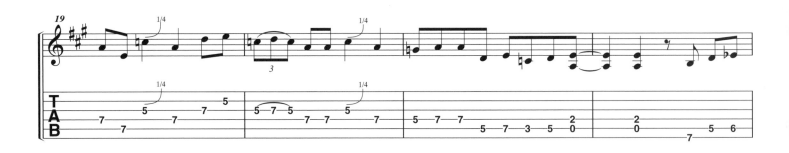

E5

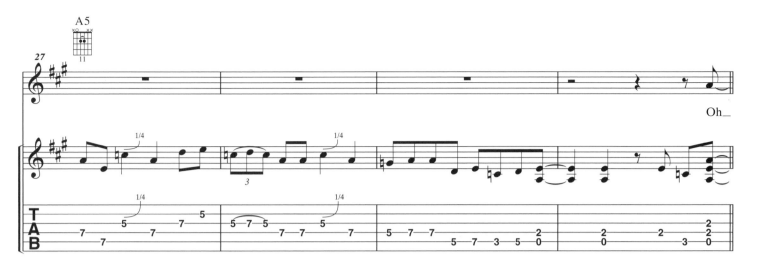

Oh__

Chorus:

___ yeah,   oh___ yeah,   ah_____ ah____ ah._____   Oh

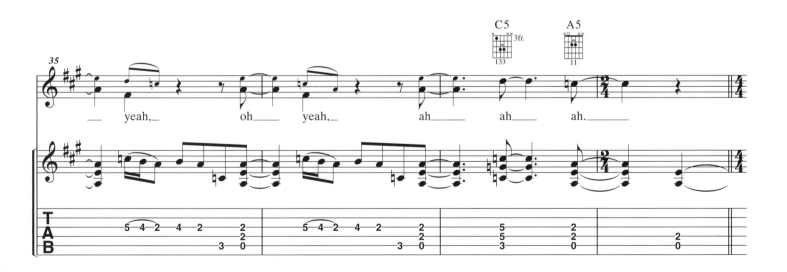

___ yeah,   oh___ yeah,   ah_____ ah____ ah._____

Verses 2 & 4:

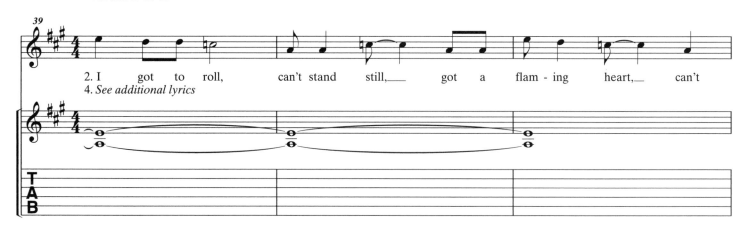

2. I got to roll, can't stand still,___ got a flam - ing heart,___ can't
4. *See additional lyrics*

get my fill.___

Elec. Gtr. 1

Elec. Gtr. 2 *(w/Leslie effect)*

mf

(2nd time only)

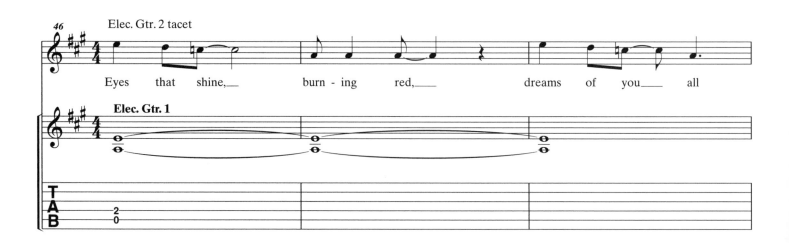

Elec. Gtr. 2 tacet

Eyes that shine,___ burn - ing red,___ dreams of you___ all

Elec. Gtr. 1

through my head._____

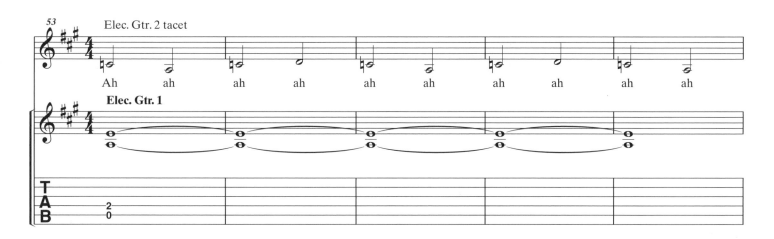

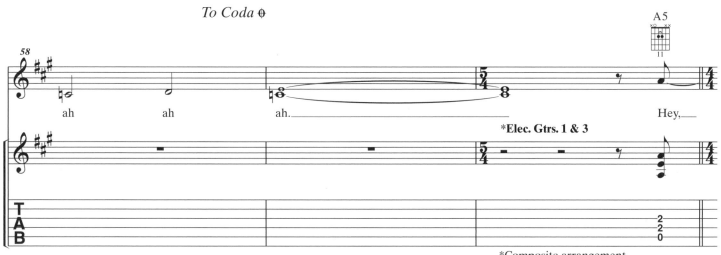

*Composite arrangement.

Verse 3:
Didn't take too long before I found out
What people mean by down and out.

Spent my money, took my car,
Started telling her friends she gonna be a star.

I don't know, but I been told,
A big-legged woman ain't got no soul.
(To Chorus:)

Verse 4:
All I ask for, all I pray,
Steady-rolling woman gonna come my way.

Need a woman gonna hold my hand
Won't tell me no lies, make me a happy man.
Ah ah ah ah ah ah ah ah ah ah ah ah ah.
(To Guitar Solo:)

BIZARRE LOVE TRIANGLE

Words and Music by
STEPHEN MORRIS, PETER HOOK,
BERNARD SUMNER and GILLIAN GILBERT

Moderately ♩ = 112

Intro:

1. Ev - 'ry__ time I__ think of you I feel a shot right through with a bolt of blue.__ It's no

2. *See additional lyrics*

prob-lem of mine_ but it's a prob-lem I find,__ liv-ing a life__ that I can't__ leave be - hind.__

There's no__ sense in__ tell-ing me__ the wis-dom of the fool won't set you free.__ But that's the

Bizarre Love Triangle - 4 - 1

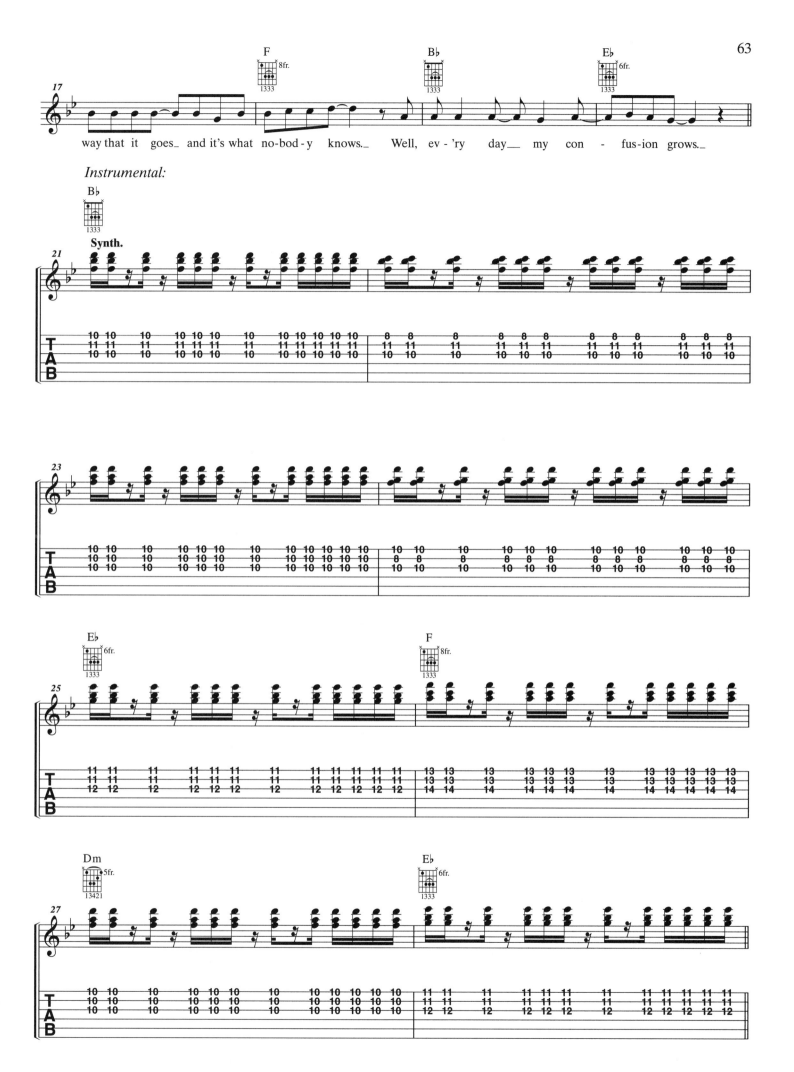

Chorus:

Verse 2:
I feel fine and I feel good,
I'm feeling like I never should.
Whenever I get this way I just don't know what to say.
Why can't we be ourselves like we were yesterday.
I'm not sure what this could mean,
I don't think you're what you seem.
I do admit to myself that, if I hurt someone else,
Then I'll never see just what we're meant to be.
(To Instrumental:)

BLITZKRIEG BOP

Words and Music by
JEFFREY HYMAN, JOHN CUMMINGS,
DOUGLAS COLVIN and THOMAS ERDELYI

Blitzkrieg Bop - 2 - 1

BORN IN THE U.S.A.

Moderately ♩ = 120

Intro:

Words and Music by
BRUCE SPRINGSTEEN

1. Born down in a dead man's town,_____ the first kick I took was when I
2.3.6. *See additional lyrics*

hit the ground._____ End up like a dog that's been beat too much,__ 'til you spend_

___ half your life just a-cov-er-ing up,_____ now.____

Chorus:
w/Rhy. Fig. 1 *(Keybds.)*

To Coda ⊕

Born in the U.S.A.___ I was born in the U.S.A.___ I was
3. *Instrumental*

Born in the U.S.A. - 2 - 1

Verse 2:
Got in a little hometown jam
So they put a rifle in my hands.
Sent me off to a foreign land
To go and kill the yellow man.
(To Chorus:)

Verse 3:
Come back home to the refinery;
Hiring man says, "Son if it was up to me."
Went down to see my V.A. man;
He said, "Son, don't you understand now?"
(To Chorus Instrumental:)

Verse 6:
Down in the shadow of the penitentiary,
Out by the gas fires of the refinery
I'm ten years burnin' down the road,
Nowhere to run, ain't got nowhere to go.
(To Chorus:)

BORN TO RUN

Words and Music by
BRUCE SPRINGSTEEN

Born to Run - 6 - 1

72

Born to Run - 6 - 4

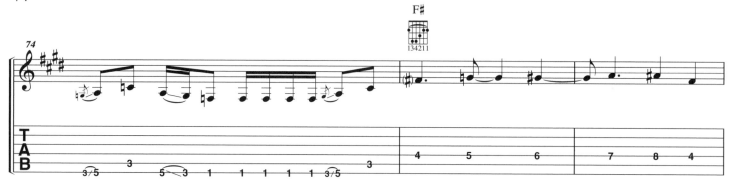

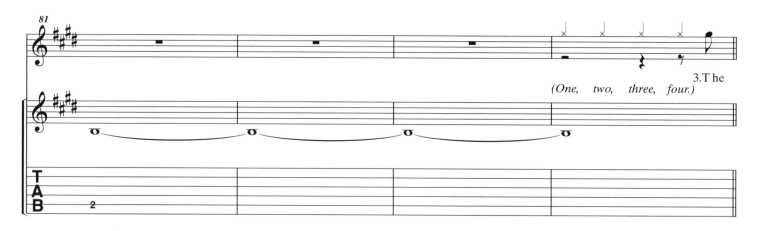

D.S. % al Coda

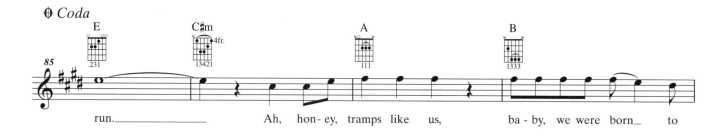

(One, two, three, four.)

3.The

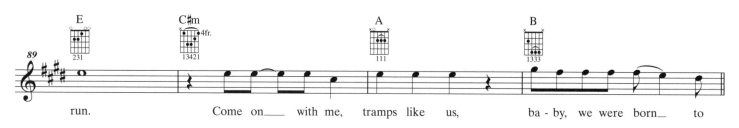

run._____ Ah, hon-ey, tramps like us, ba-by, we were born_ to

run._____ Come on___ with me, tramps like us, ba-by, we were born_ to

Outro:

w/Rhy. Fig. 1 *(Elec. Gtr. 1) 2 times*

Verse 2:
Wendy, let me in, I wanna be your friend,
I want to guard your dreams and visions.
Just wrap your legs 'round these velvet rims
And strap your hands across my engines.
Together we could break this trap,
We'll run 'til we drop, baby, we'll never go back.
Will you walk with me out on the wire,
'Cause, baby, I'm just a scared and lonely rider.
But I gotta find out how it feels,
I want to know if love is wild, girl, I want to know if love is real.
(To Saxophone Solo:)

Verse 3:
The highway's jammed with broken heroes
On a last chance power drive.
Everybody's out on the run tonight but there's no place left to hide.
Together, Wendy, we can live with the sadness,
I'll love you with all the madness in my soul.
Someday, girl, I don't know when, we're gonna get to that place
Where we really want to go and well walk in the sun.
But 'til then, tramps like us, baby, we were born to run.
Ah, honey, tramps like us, baby, we were born to run.
Come on with me, tramps like us, baby, we were born to run.
(To Outro:)

THE BOYS OF SUMMER

Words and Music by
DON HENLEY and MIKE CAMPBELL

To match record key, tune down a half step

Bright ♩ = 168

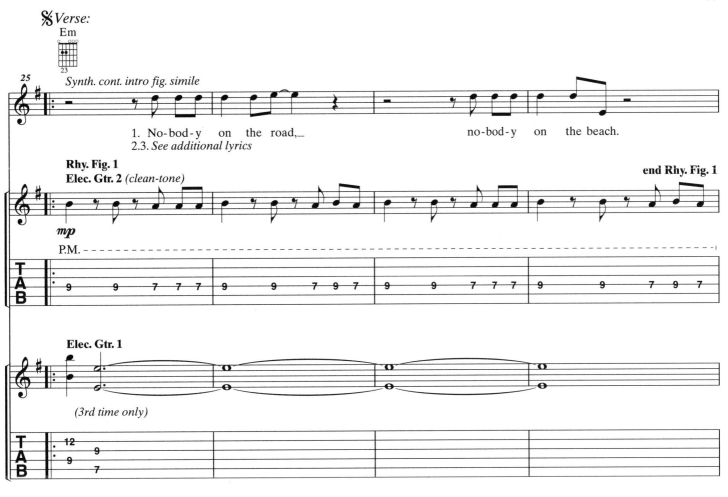

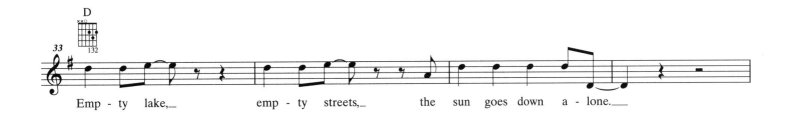

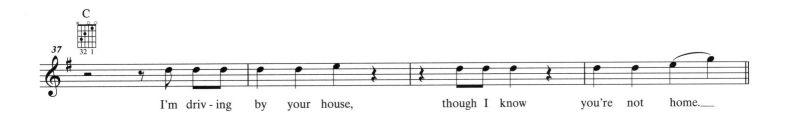

Chorus:

But I can see you,____ your brown skin

Elec. Gtr. 3 *(clean-tone)*

mp *hold throughout*

shin- ing in the sun.____

You got your hair combed back and your
I see you walk-in' real slow and your
You got the top pulled down and that

sun- glass- es on, ba- by.
smil- ing at ev- 'ry- one.
ra- di- o on, ba- by.

Elec. Gtr. 3 cont. simile

And I can tell you my

To Coda ⊕

love for you will still be strong af- ter____ the boys____ of

The Boys of Summer - 6 - 3

D.S. ℅ al Coda

Coda

Elec. Gtr. 3 cont. chorus fig. simile

sum - mer___ have gone.___ I can see you,___ your brown skin shin - ing in the sun.___ You got that hair slicked back and those Way - far - ers on, ba - by. And I can tell you my love for you will still be strong af - ter___ the boys___ of sum - mer___ have gone.___

Outro:

Repeat and fade

Verse 2:
I never will forget those nights,
I wonder if it was a dream.
Remember how you made me crazy?
Remember how I made you scream?
Now I don't understand what's happened
To our love,
But, babe, I'm gonna get you back,
I'm gonna show you what I'm made of.
(To Chorus:)

Verse 3:
Out on the road today I saw a Deadhead sticker
On a Cadillac.
A little voice inside my head said,
Don't look back. you can never look back.
I thought I knew what love was,
What did I know?
Those days are gone forever,
I should just let them go but...
(To Chorus:)

BROWN SUGAR

Words and Music by
MICK JAGGER and KEITH RICHARDS

Moderately ♩ = 126

Intro:

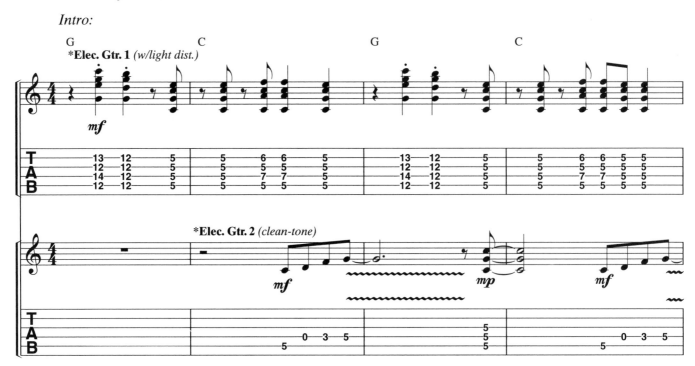

*Elec. Gtrs. 1 & 2 are both in open G tuning: ⑥ = D; ⑤ = G; ④ = D; ③ = G; ② = B; ① = D

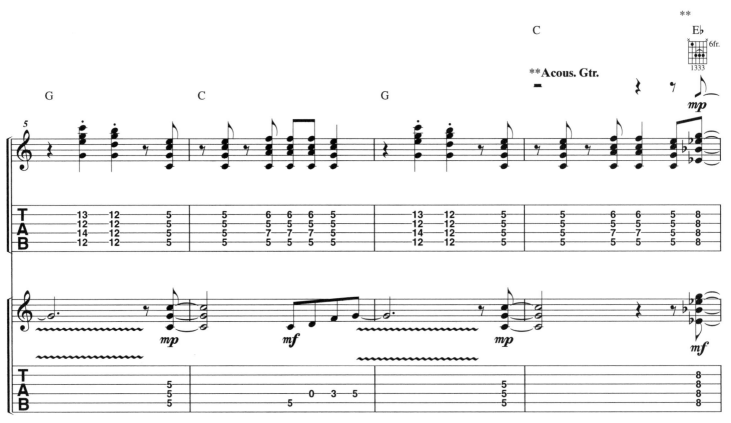

**Chord frames reflect Acous. Gtr. in standard tuning, entering at meas. 8.

Brown Sugar - 7 - 1

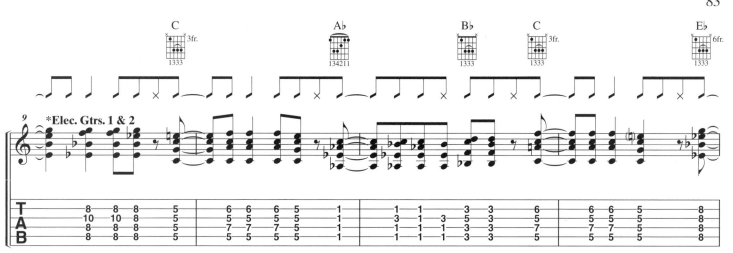

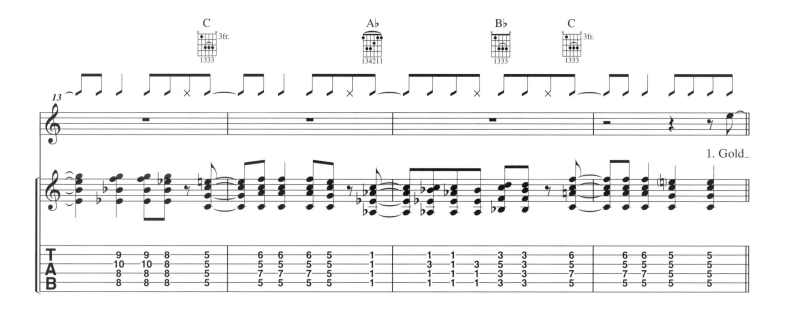

*Composite arrangement.

2.3. *See additional lyrics*

Verse 2:
Drums beating, cold English blood runs hot,
Lady of the house wondrin' where it's gonna stop.
House boy knows that he's doin' alright,
You should a heard him just around midnight.
(To Chorus:)

Verse 3:
I bet your mama was a tent show queen,
And all her boyfriends were sweet sixteen.
I'm no schoolboy but I know what I like,
You should have heard me just around midnight.
(To Chorus:)

COMFORTABLY NUMB

Words and Music by
ROGER WATERS and DAVID GILMOUR

Moderately slow ♩ = 64

1. Hel-lo, hel-lo, hel-lo,___ is there an-y-bod-y in there? Just nod if you can hear me. Is there an-y-one___ home?

Come on, come on now,___ I hear you're feel-ing___ down.___ Well,
2. O-kay, o-kay,___ just a lit-tle pin-prick.___ There'll be no more,

I can ease your pain,___ get you on your feet a-gain.___
(Ahh.)___ but you might feel a lit-tle sick.___ Can you

Comfortably Numb - 5 - 1

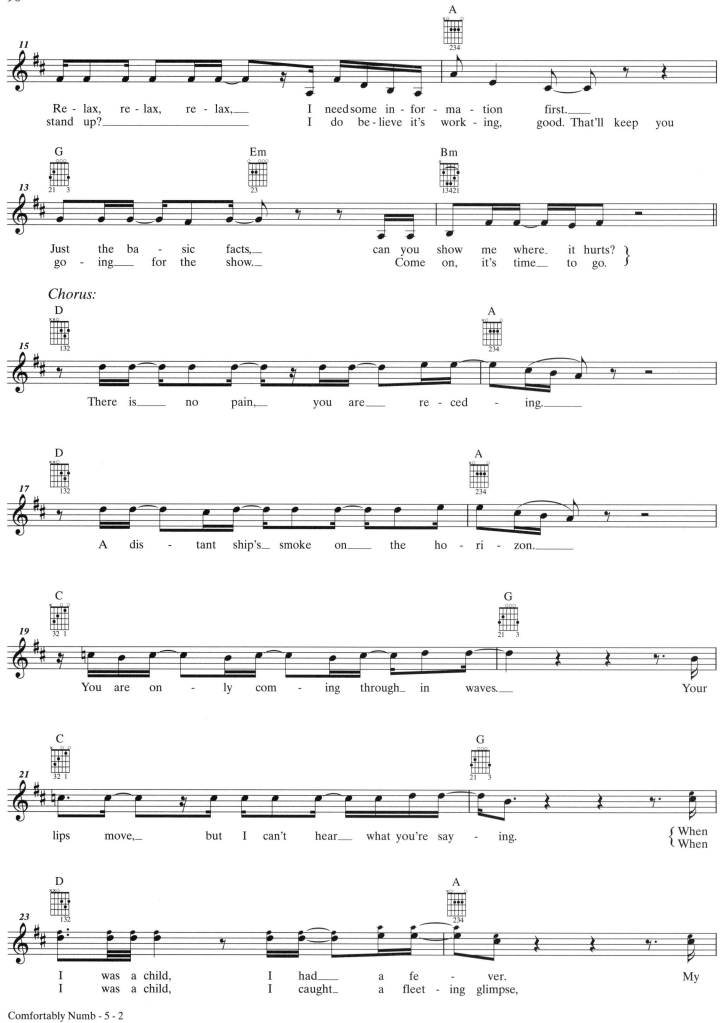

COME TOGETHER

Words and Music by
JOHN LENNON and
PAUL McCARTNEY

Moderately slow ♩ = 83

Intro:

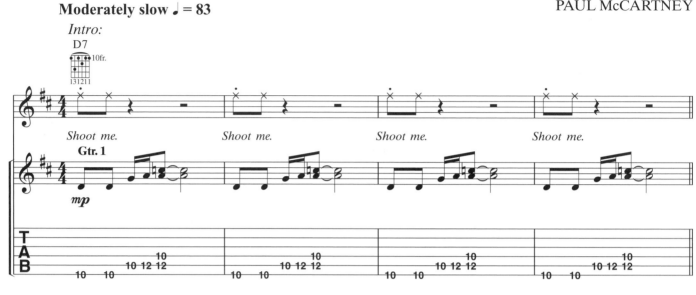

Verse 1:

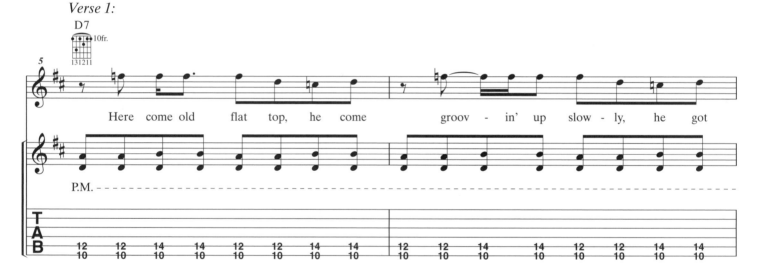

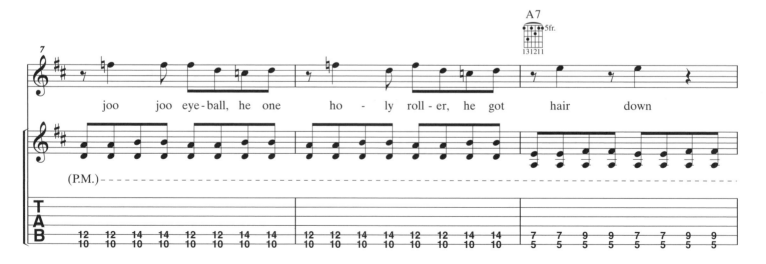

Come Together - 6 - 1

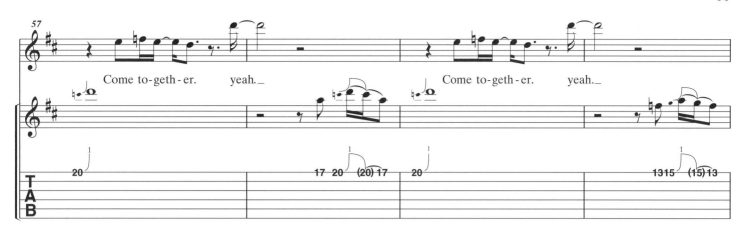

Come to-geth-er. yeah.___ Come to-geth-er. yeah.___

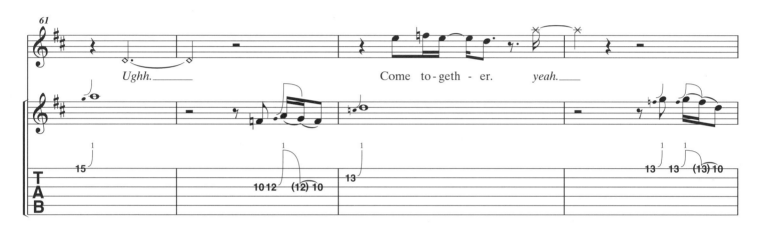

Ughh._____ Come to-geth-er. yeah.___

Repeat ad lib. and fade

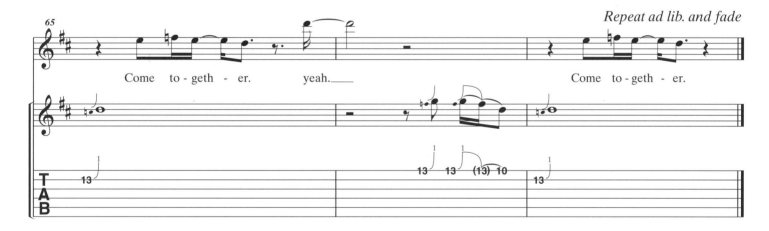

Come to-geth-er. yeah.___ Come to-geth-er.

Verse 3:
He Bag Production, he got walrus gumboot,
He got Ono sideboard, he one spinal cracker,
He got feet down below his knee.
Hold you in his armchair, you can feel his disease.
(To Chorus:)

Verse 4:
He roller coaster, he got early warnin',
He got muddy water, he one mojo filter,
He say, "One and one and one is three."
Got to be good lookin' 'cause he's so hard to see.
(To Chorus:)

FAKE PLASTIC TREES

Words and Music by
THOMAS YORKE, EDWARD O'BRIEN,
COLIN GREENWOOD,
JONATHAN GREENWOOD
and PHILIP SELWAY

FAMILY AFFAIR

Words and Music by
SYLVESTER STEWART

Family Affair - 4 - 1

Instrumental:

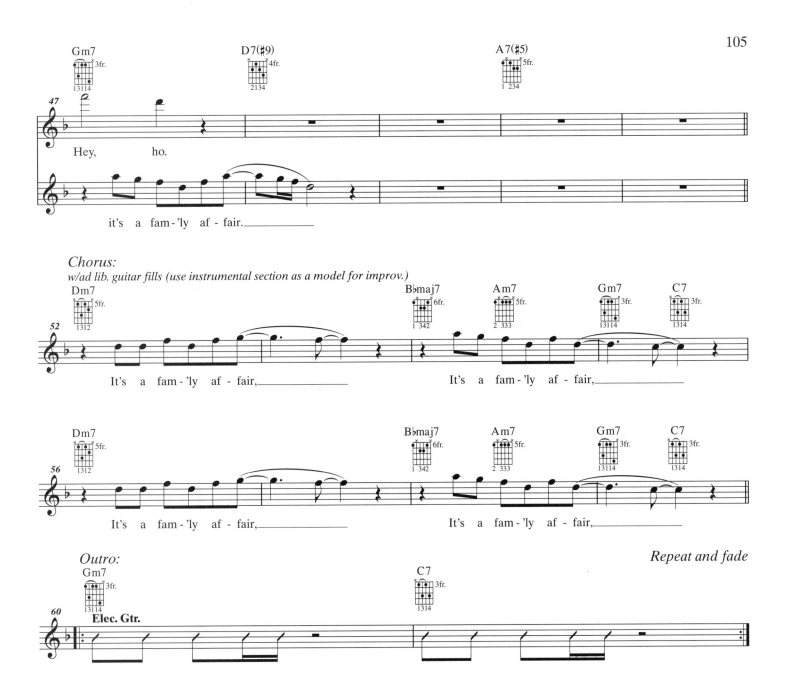

Verse 2:
Newlywed a year ago
But you're still checking each other out, hey, hey.
Nobody wants to blow,
Nobody wants to be left out.
You can't leave, 'cause your heart is there.
But you can't stay, 'cause you been somewhere else.
You can't cry, 'cause you'll look broke down.
But you're cryin' anyway 'cause you're all broke down.
It's a family affair...
(To Coda)

FAST CAR

To match record key, Capo II

Moderately ♩ = 104

Words and Music by
TRACY CHAPMAN

1. You got a fast____ car, I want a tick-et to an-y-where.
2.3. See additional lyrics

May - be we can make a deal, may - be to-geth-er we can get some - where.___

An - y place is bet - ter,___ start - ing from zer - o, got noth - ing to lose.

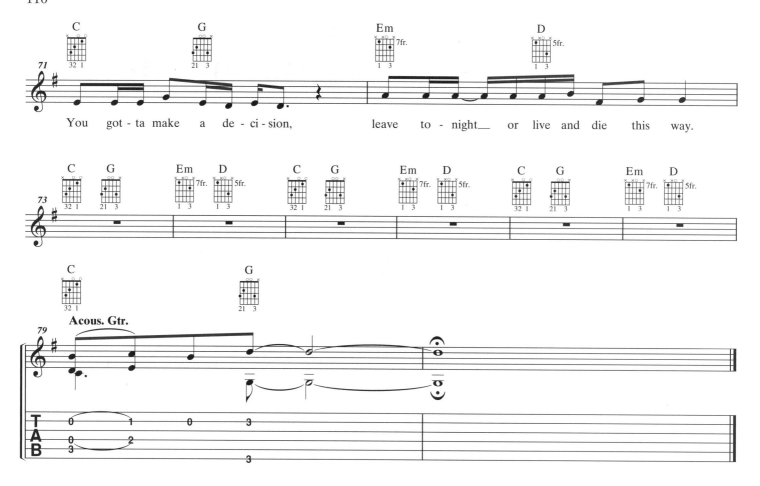

You got - ta make a de - ci - sion, leave to - night___ or live and die this way.

Acous. Gtr.

Verse 2:
You got a fast car,
I got a plan to get us out of here.
Been working at the convenience store,
Managed to save just a little bit of money.
We won't have to drive too far,
Just 'cross the border and into the city.
You and I can both get jobs,
And finally see what it means to be living.

Verse 3:
See my old man's got a problem,
He lives with the bottle, that's the way it is.
He says his body's too old for working,
His body's too young to look like his.
My mama went off and left him,
She wanted more from life than he could give.
I said, somebody's got to take care of him,
So I quit school and that's what I did.
(To Verse 4:)

Verse 6:
You got a fast car,
I got a job that pays all our bills.
You stay out drinking late at the bar,
See more of your friends than you do of your kids.
I'd always hoped for better,
Thought maybe together you and me would find it.
I got no plans, I ain't going nowhere,
So take your fast car and keep on driving.
(To Bridge:)

GET UP
(I FEEL LIKE BEING A) SEX MACHINE

Words and Music by
JAMES BROWN, BOBBY BYRD
and RONALD LENHOFF

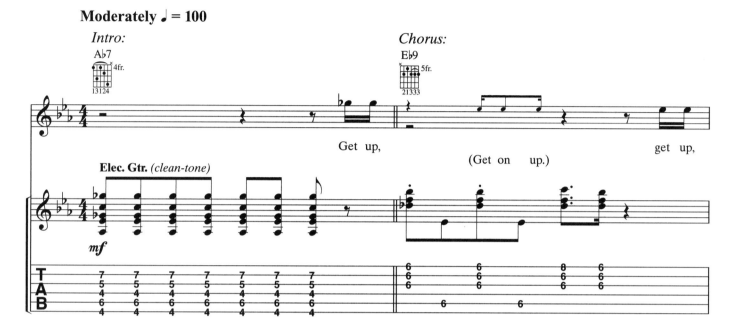

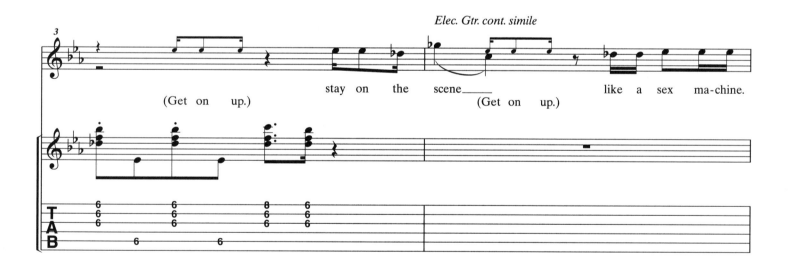

Get Up (I Feel Like Being a) Sex Machine - 5 - 1

Verse 1:

Chorus:

Chorus:

GIMME SHELTER

Words and Music by
MICK JAGGER and KEITH RICHARDS

Gimme Shelter - 5 - 1

Guitar Solo:

yeah,___ yeah,___ yeah.___

Coda

Chorus:

fade___ a - way.___ War,___ chil - dren,___

it's just a shot a - way,___ it's just a shot a - way.___ It's just a shot a - way,___

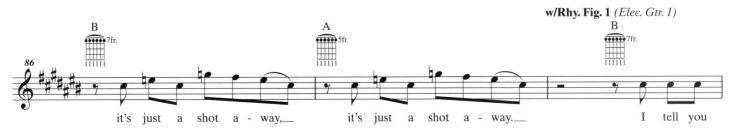

it's just a shot a - way,___ it's just a shot a - way.___ I tell you

love,___ sis - ter,___ it's just a kiss a - way,_ it's just a kiss a - way._

It's just a kiss a - way,_ it's just a kiss a - way,_ it's just a kiss a-way, kiss a-way, kiss a - way.___

Outro:

Repeat and fade

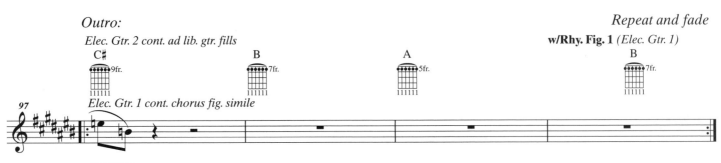

GRACELAND

Words and Music by
PAUL SIMON

Bright in 2 ♩ = 120

Intro:

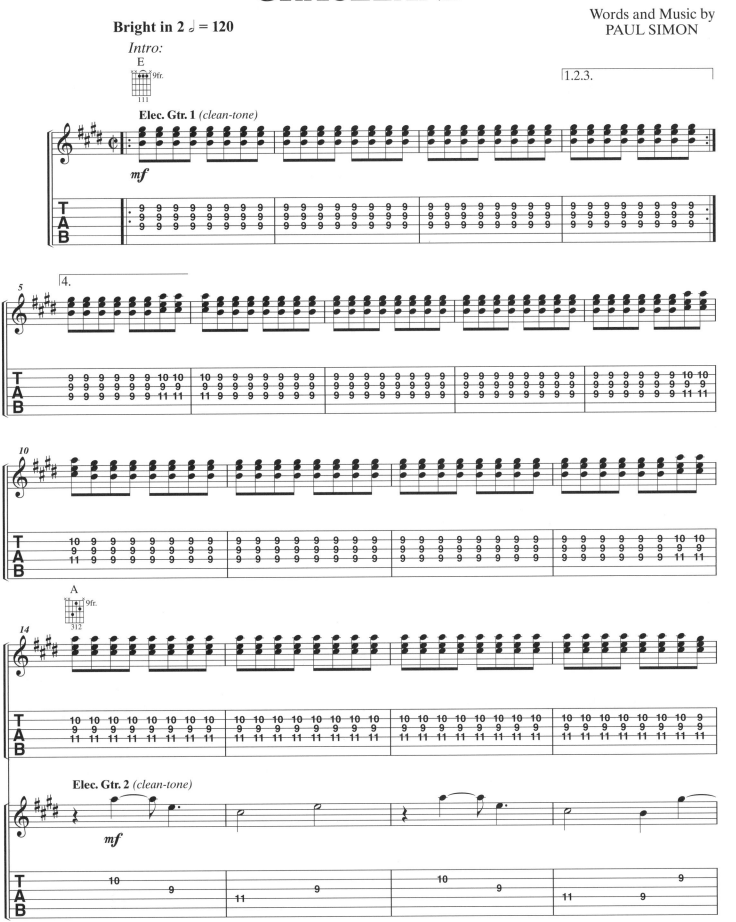

Graceland - 7 - 1

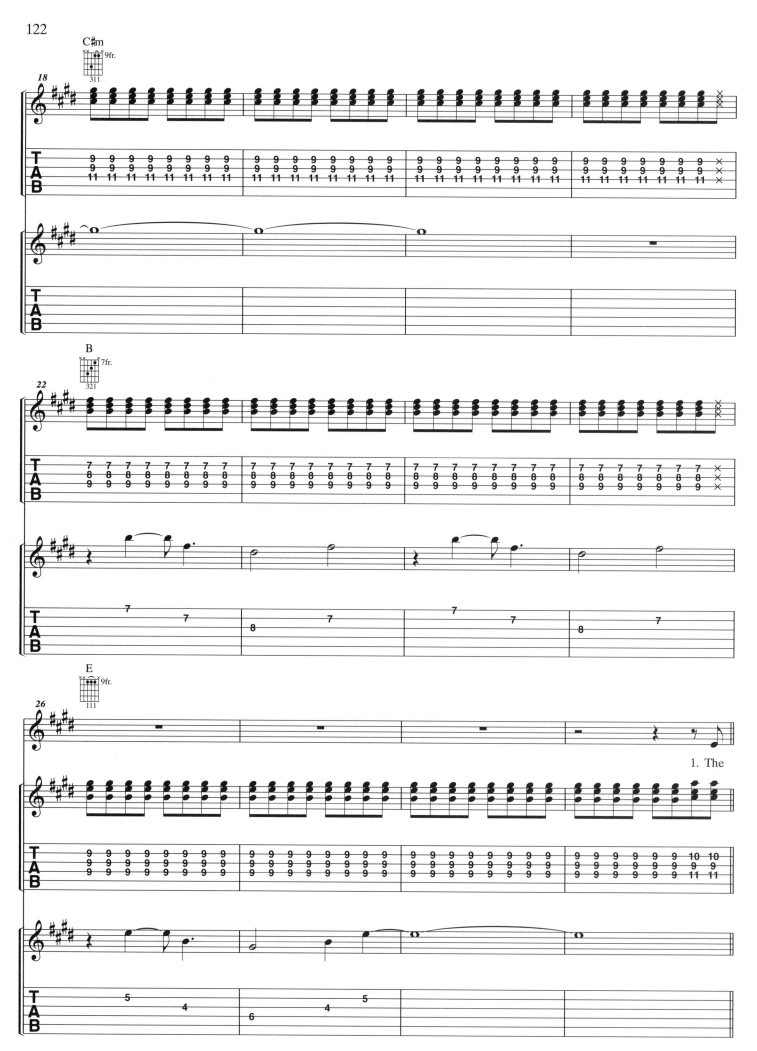

Verses 2 & 4:

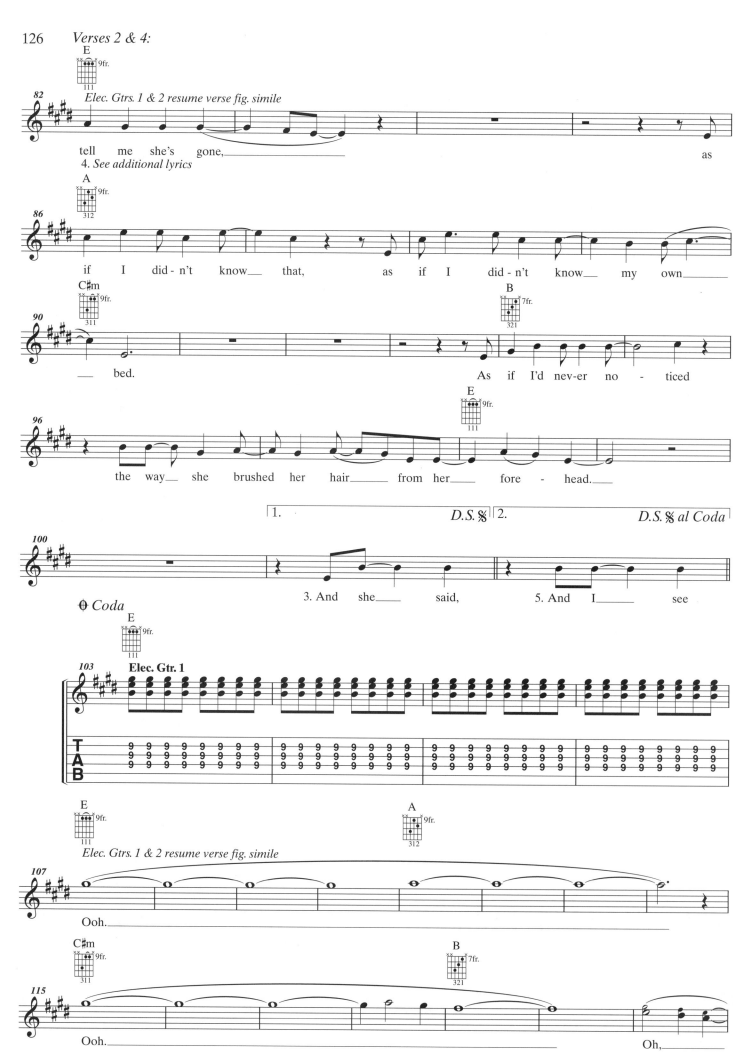

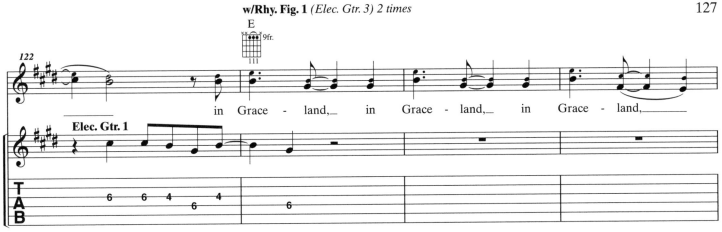

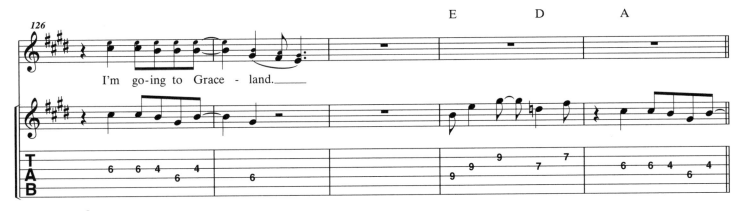

Outro:

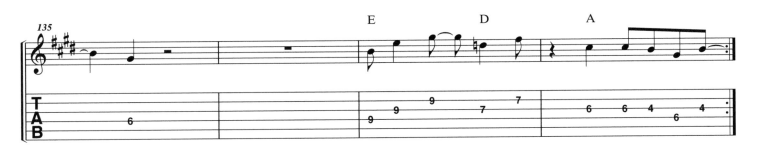

Verse 3:
And she said losing love
Is like a window in your heart.
Everybody sees you're blown apart,
Everybody sees the wind blow.

Chorus 2:
I'm going to Graceland, in Memphis, Tennessee,
I'm going to Graceland…
Poorboys and Pilgrims with families
And we are going to Graceland.
And my traveling companions
Are ghosts and empty sockets,
I'm looking at ghosts and empties.
But I've reason to believe
We all will be received in Graceland.

Verse 4:
There is a girl in New York City,
Who calls herself the human trampoline.
And sometimes when I'm falling, flying
Or tumbling in turmoil I say,
Whoa, so this is what she means.
She means we're bouncing into
Graceland.

Verse 5:
And I see losing love
Is like a window in your heart.
Everybody sees you're blown apart,
Everybody feels the wind blow.

Chorus 3:
In Graceland, Graceland,
I'm going to Graceland…
For reasons I cannot explain
There's some part of me wants to see
 Graceland.
And I may be obliged to defend
Every love, every ending,
Or maybe there's no obligations now.
Maybe I've a reason to believe
We all will be received in Graceland.
(To Outro:)

GO YOUR OWN WAY

Capo III ⟶ D   A   G   Bm

Frames for Acous. Gtr. w/capo III.

Words and Music by
LINDSEY BUCKINGHAM

Moderately ♩ = 136

Intro:

*Italic chord names represent Acous. Gtr. w/capo III.
Frames for Acous. Gtr. appear under song title.

**Acous. Gtr. w/capo III. TAB numbers relative to capo.

Verse:

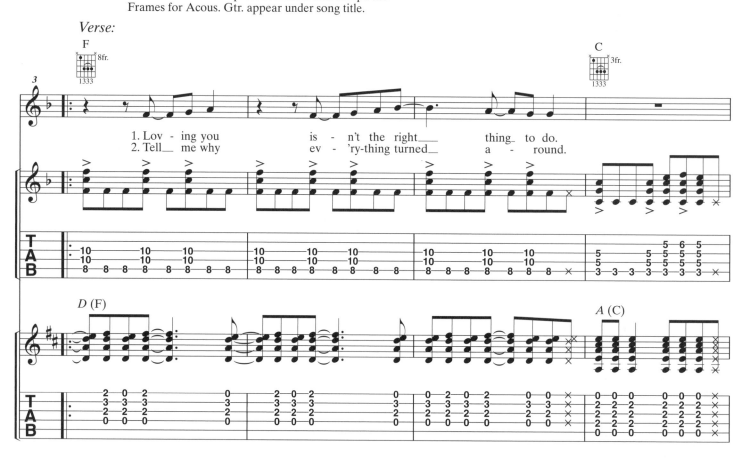

1. Lov - ing you   is - n't the right___ thing__ to do.
2. Tell__ me why   ev - 'ry-thing turned__ a - round.

Go Your Own Way - 4 - 1

Go Your Own Way - 4 - 2

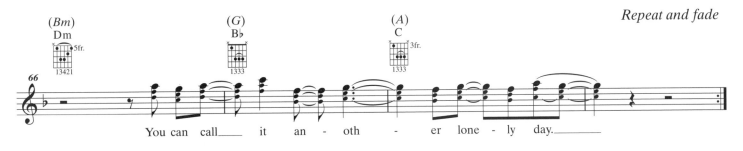

GOD SAVE THE QUEEN

Words and Music by
PAUL COOK, STEVE JONES,
GLEN MATLOCK and JOHNNY ROTTEN

Moderately fast ♩ = 140

Intro:

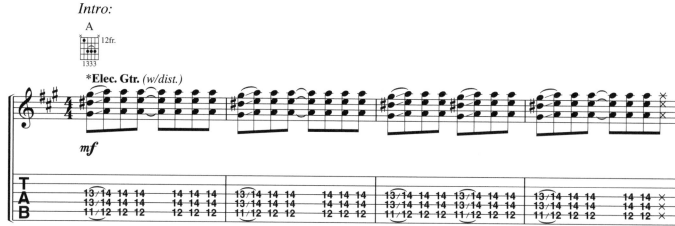

*Composite arrangement.

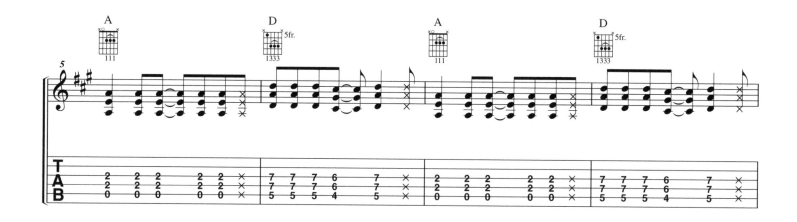

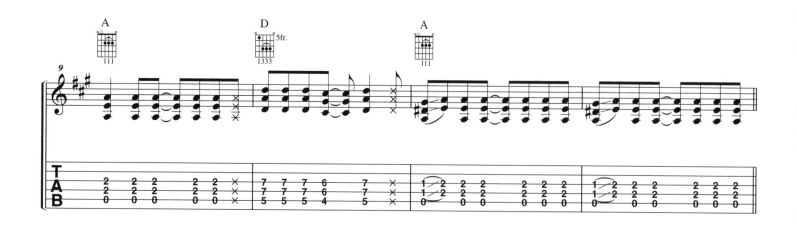

God Save the Queen - 6 - 1

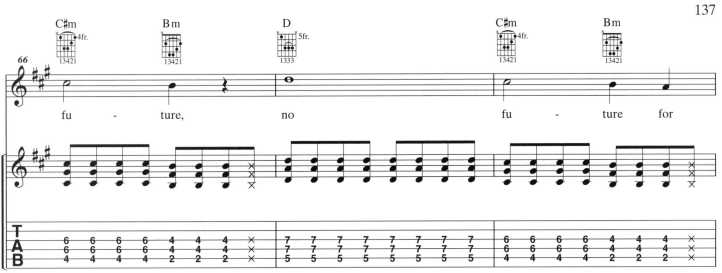

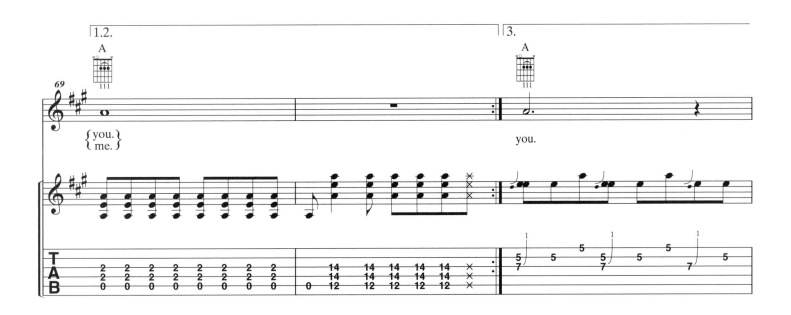

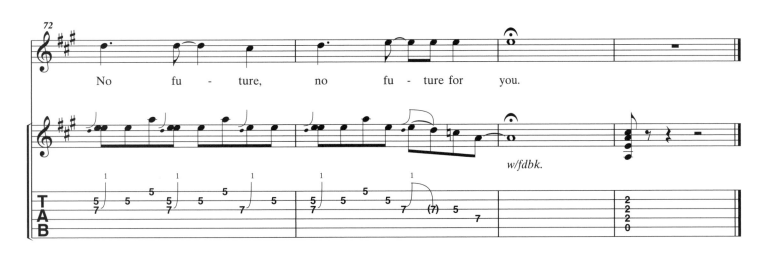

God Save the Queen - 6 - 6

GOOD TIMES

Words and Music by
BERNARD EDWARDS and NILE RODGERS

Good Times - 2 - 1

HEARTBREAKER

Music and Lyrics by
JIMMY PAGE, ROBERT PLANT,
JOHN PAUL JONES and JOHN BONHAM

Moderately ♩ = 98

Intro:

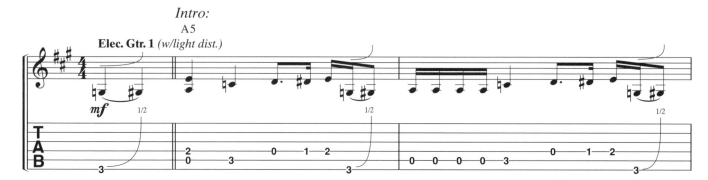

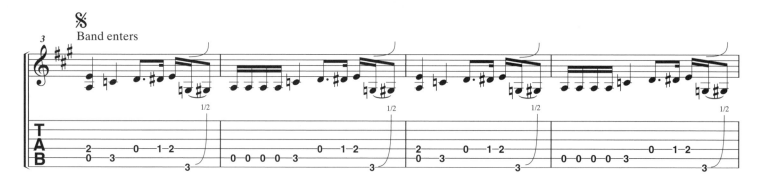

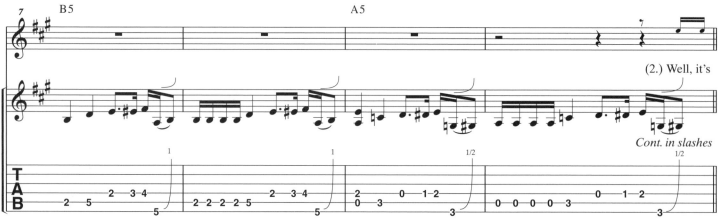

Verses 1 & 2:

1. Hey, fel - las, have you heard the news,_ you know that An-nie's back_ in town._ It
(2.) been ten years_ or may - be more_____ since I first set eyes_ on you._ The

*Composite arrangement. **Chord names without frames implied by bass gtr.

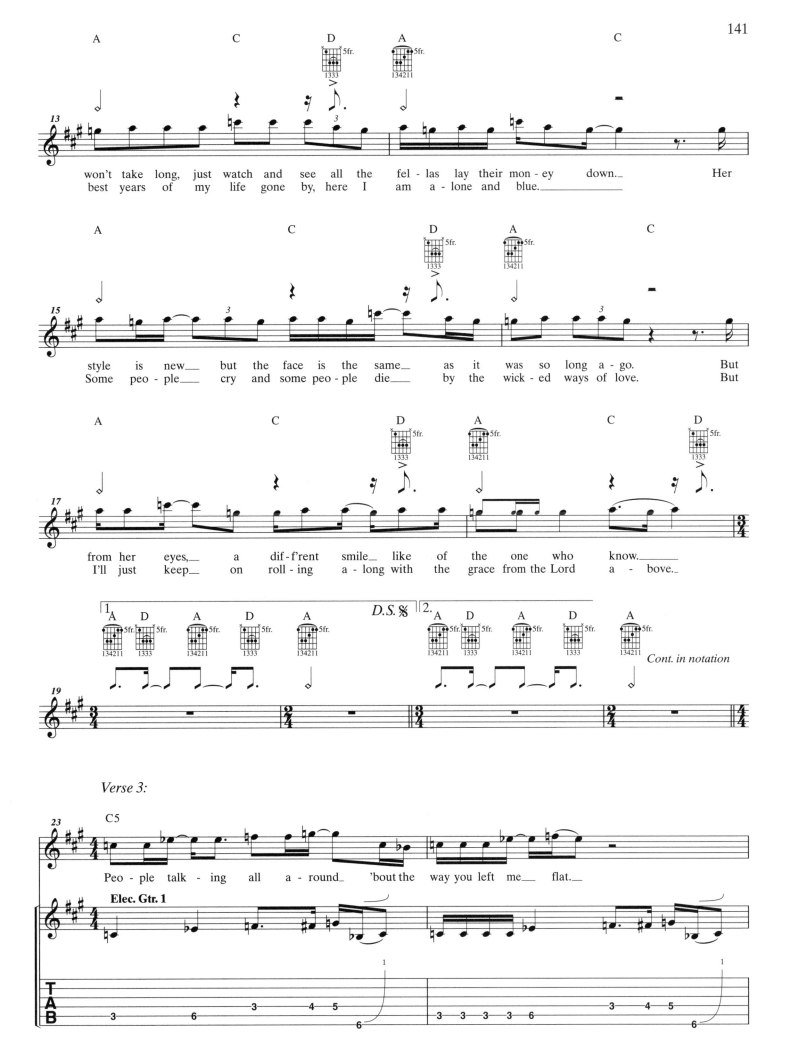

Elec. Gtrs. 1 & 2

Elec. Gtr. 1 cont. in notation

___ no use.___   Give it   to me,   give it.

Freetime

A

Elec. Gtr. 1

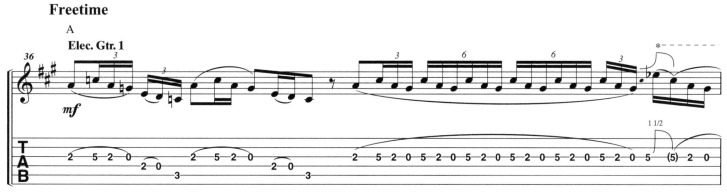

*Bend strings behind nut w/r.h.

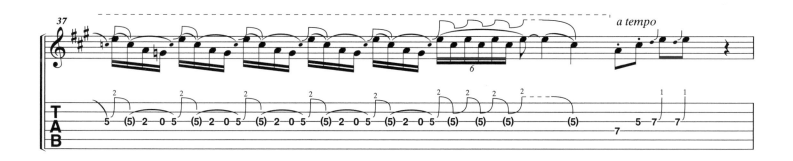

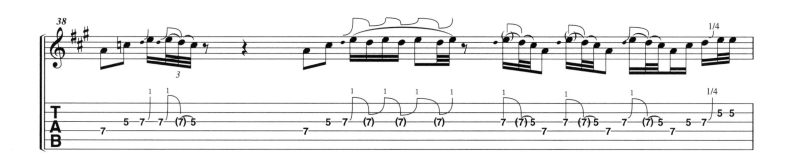

Interlude:

Dbl. time ♩ = **196**

N.C.

Band enters

A5

11

Elec. Gtr. 1

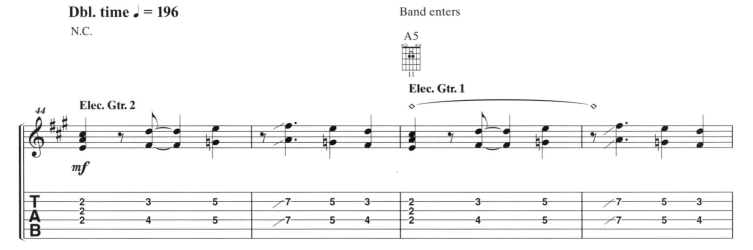

Elec. Gtr. 2

mf

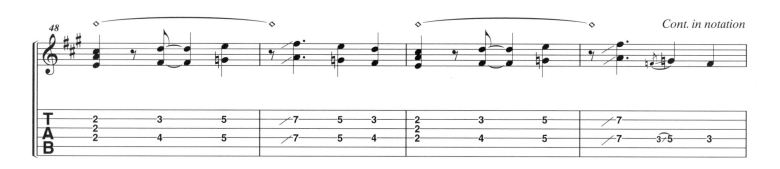

Cont. in notation

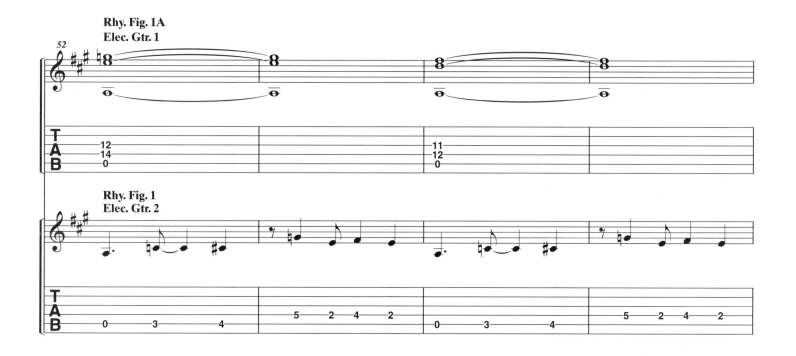

Rhy. Fig. 1A
Elec. Gtr. 1

Rhy. Fig. 1
Elec. Gtr. 2

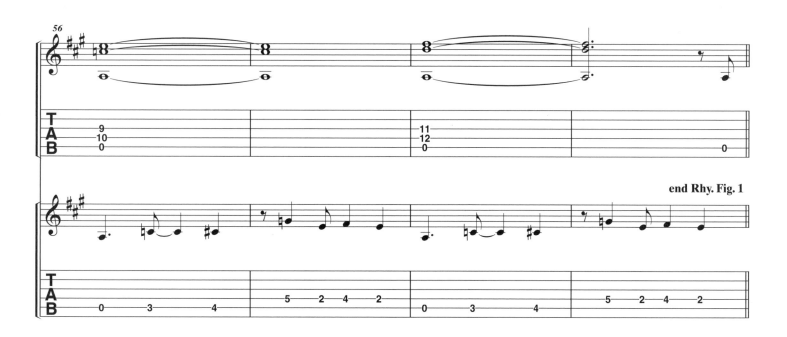

end Rhy. Fig. 1

Guitar Solo 2:
w/Rhy. Fig. 1 *(Elec. Gtr. 2) 2 times*

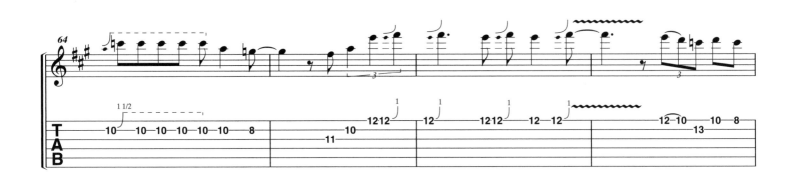

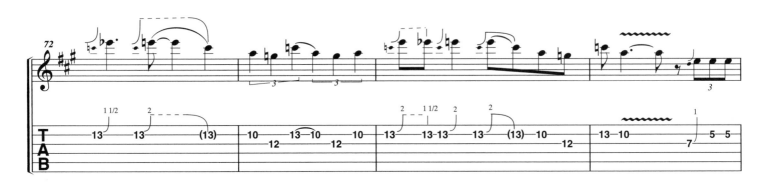

Verse 4:

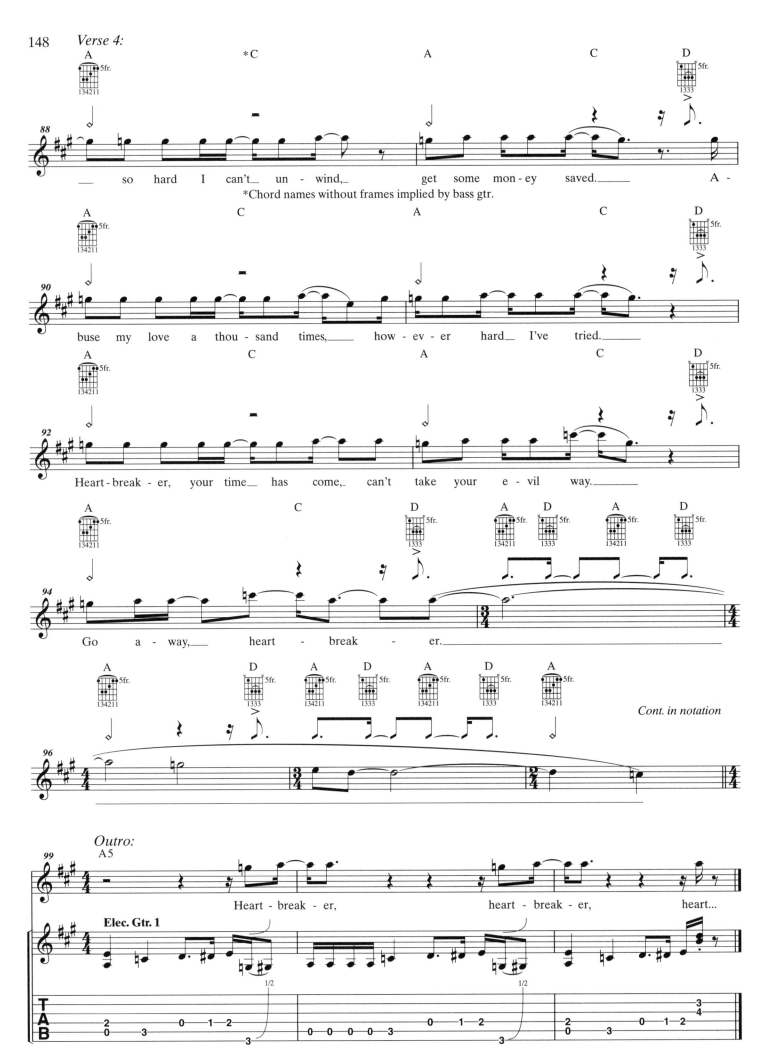

*Chord names without frames implied by bass gtr.

so hard I can't__ un - wind,__ get some mon - ey saved.____ A -

buse my love a thou - sand times,____ how - ev - er hard__ I've tried.____

Heart - break - er, your time__ has come,_ can't take your e - vil way._____

Go a - way,__ heart - break - er._____

Cont. in notation

Outro:

A5

Heart - break - er, heart - break - er, heart...

Elec. Gtr. 1

IRON MAN

Words and Music by
FRANK IOMMI, JOHN OSBOURNE,
WILLIAM WARD and TERENCE BUTLER

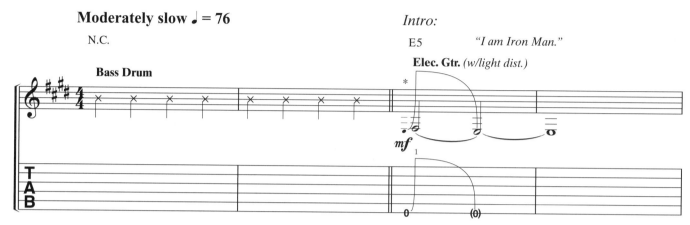

*Strike open string and push string down behind nut
bending it one whole step and gradually release.

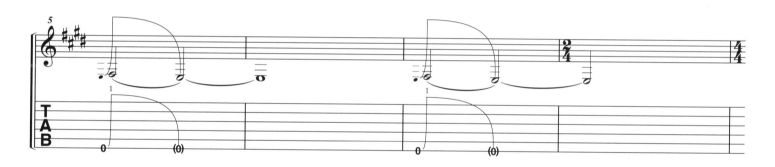

Iron Man - 7 - 1

Verse 1:

Has he lost his mind? Can he see or is he blind?

Can he walk at all? Or, if he moves,___ will he fall?

w/Riff A *(Elec. Gtr.) 1st 2 meas. only*

Verse 2:

w/Riff B *(Elec. Gtr.)*

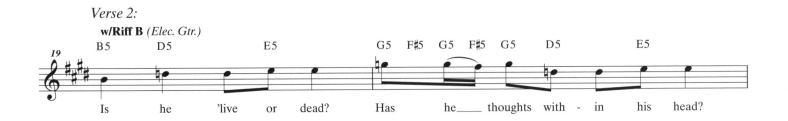

Is he 'live or dead? Has he___ thoughts with - in his head?

We'll just pass him there. Why should_ we___ e - ven care?

Interlude:

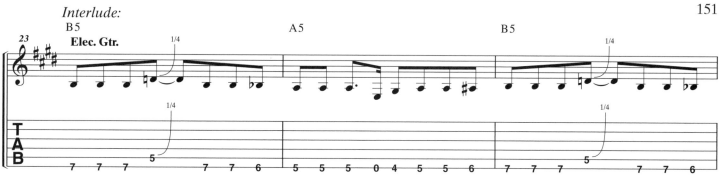

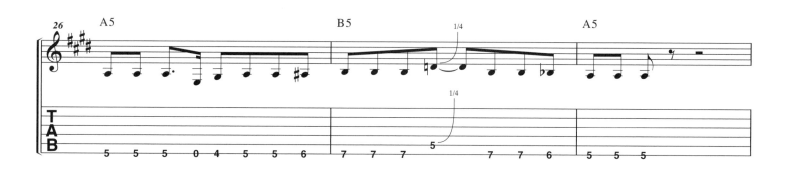

w/Riff A *(Elec. Gtr.)*

Verses 3 & 4:
w/Riff B *(Elec. Gtr.)*

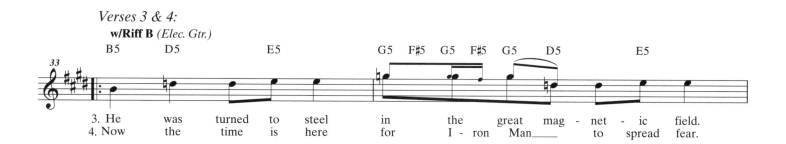

3. He was turned to steel in the great mag - net - ic field.
4. Now the time is here for I - ron Man____ to spread fear.

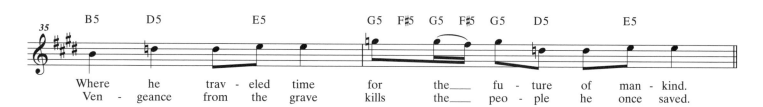

Where he trav - eled time for the____ fu - ture of man - kind.
Ven - geance from the grave kills the____ peo - ple he once saved.

Chorus:

No-bod-y wants_ him,_   he__ just stares_ at the world.
No-bod-y wants_ him,_   they_ just turn_ their_ heads.

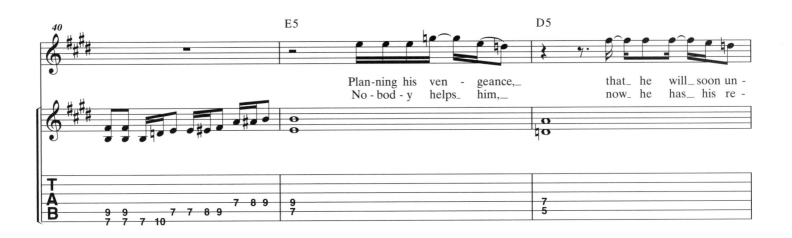

Plan-ning his ven - geance,_   that_ he will_ soon un -
No - bod - y helps_ him,_   now_ he has_ his re -

1.

fold.
venge.

w/Riff A *(Elec. Gtr.)*

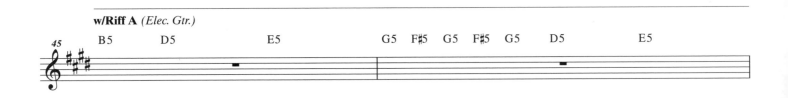

Half time ♩ = 76

Interlude:

w/**Riff A** *(Elec. Gtr.)*

Verse 5:
w/**Riff B** *(Elec. Gtr.)*

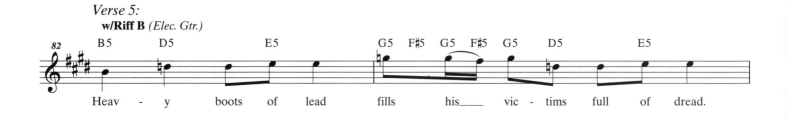

Heav - y boots of lead fills his___ vic - tims full of dread.

Run - ning as fast as they can, I - ron___ Man___ lives a - gain!___

Iron Man - 7 - 6

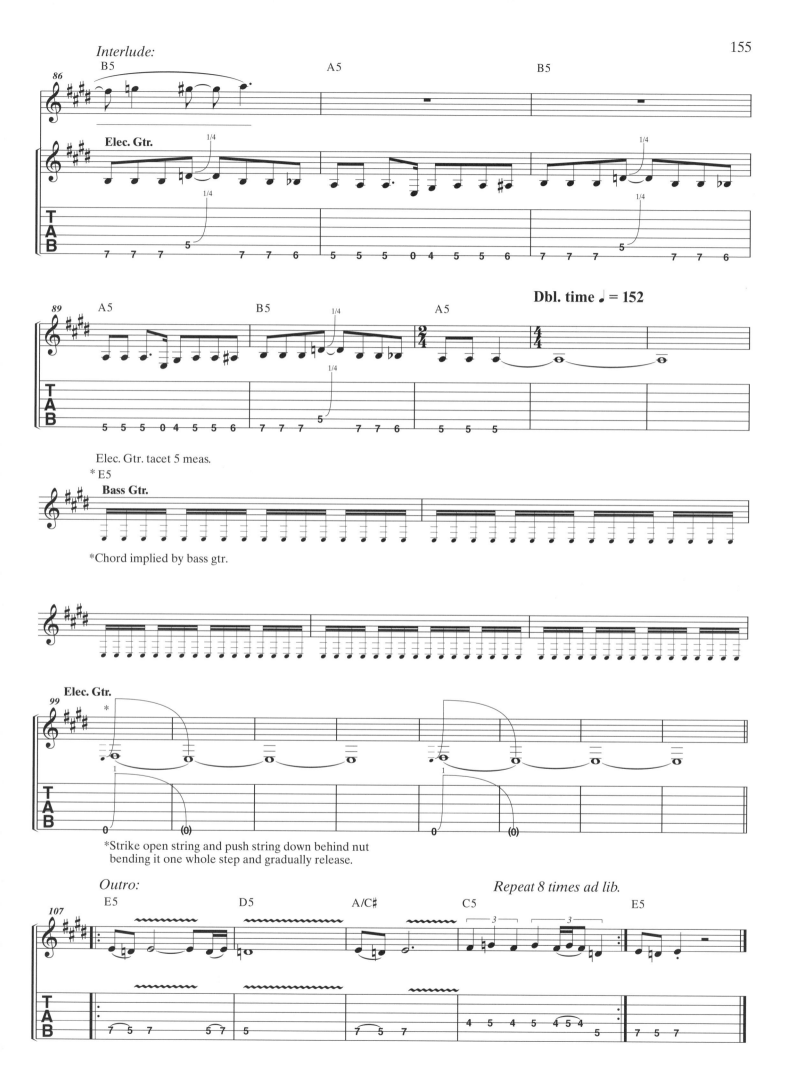

HIGHWAY TO HELL

Words and Music by
ANGUS YOUNG, MALCOLM YOUNG
and BON SCOTT

Moderately ♩ = 120

Intro:
Drums enter 2nd time.

Elec. Gtr. 1 (w/light dist.)
Rhy. Fig. 1

end Rhy. Fig. 1

*Two gtrs. arr. for one.

Verse:
w/Rhy. Fig. 1 *(Elec. Gtr. 1) 3 times*

8va throughout

1. Liv - in' eas - y, liv - in' free, sea - son tick - et on a
2. No stop signs, speed lim - it, no - bod - y's gon - na

one way ride. Ask - ing noth - ing, leave me be,
slow me down. Like a wheel, gon - na spin it,

tak - ing ev - 'ry - thing in my stride. Don't need rea - son,
no - bod - 's gon - na mess me 'round, Hey Sa - tan,

don't need rhyme, ain't noth - in' that I'd rath - er do.
paid my dues, play - in' in a rock - in' band.

2.

HOTEL CALIFORNIA

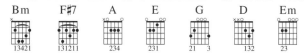

Chord frames reflecting concert key (for uncapoed gtr.)

Words and Music by
DON HENLEY, GLENN FREY
and DON FELDER

Moderately slow ♩ = 74

Intro:

Acous. Gtr. 1 w/capo VII, transposed to E minor.
Chord frames and TAB numbers relative to capo.
All other guitars w/o capo.
Chord frames w/italic names above represent capoed gtr.
Non-italic chord names under frames represent concert key.
Chord frames reflecting concert key appear under song title.

Hotel California - 10 - 1

Verses 1 & 2:

w/Rhy. Fig. 1 *(Acous. Gtr. 1) 2 times, simile*

1. On a dark des-ert high - way,_ cool_ wind in my hair,
2. Her mind is Tif - fan-y twist - ed._ She got the Mer - ce - des bends.

Rhy. Fig. 1A
Elec. Gtr. 1 *(clean-tone)*

mf P.M. throughout

warm_ smell_ of co - li - tas_ ris - ing up through the air.____
She got a lot of pret-ty, pret - ty boys that she calls friends.____

Hotel California - 10 - 4

Guitar Solo:

w/Rhy. Figs. 1 *(Acous. Gtr. 1)* **& 1A** *(Elec. Gtr. 1) both 3 times, simile*

Hotel California - 10 - 8

Outro:

w/Rhy. Figs. 1 (Acous. Gtr. 1) & 1A (Elec. Gtr. 1) both simile

Elec. Gtr. 4

Elec. Gtr. 3

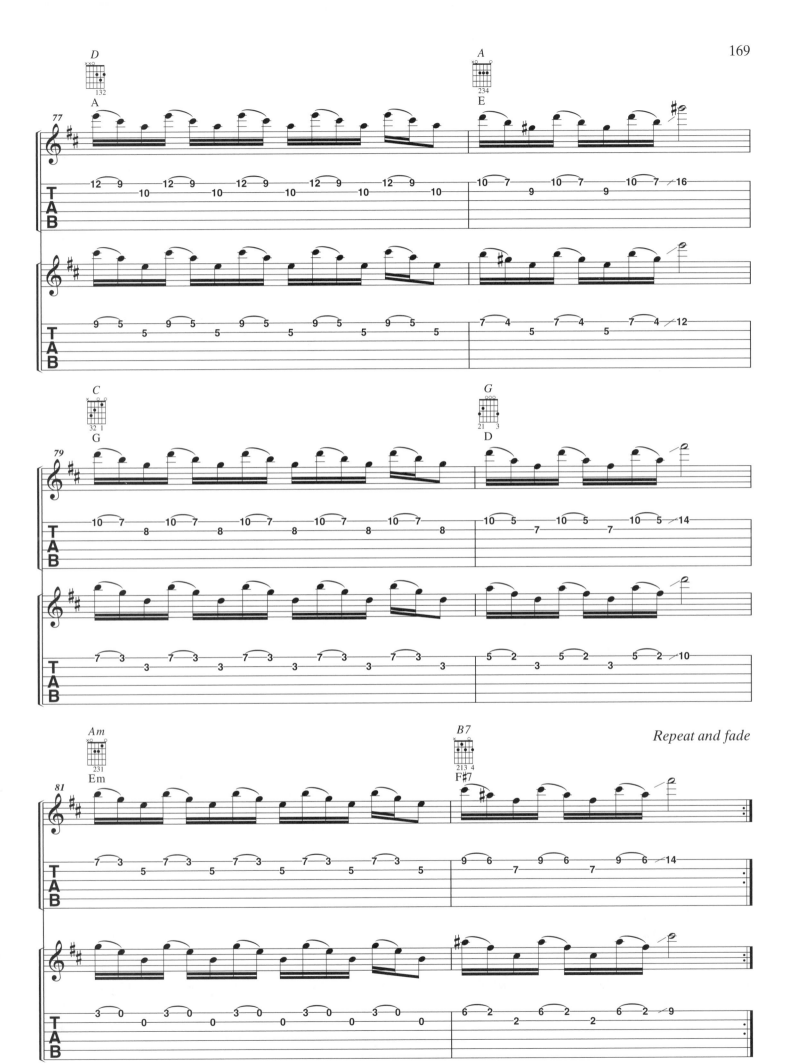

Repeat and fade

Hotel California - 10 - 10

I WANNA BE SEDATED

Moderately fast ♩ = 160

Intro:

Words and Music by
JEFFREY HYMAN, JOHN CUMMINGS
and DOUGLAS COLVIN

INTO THE MYSTIC

To match record key, Capo III

Moderately slow ♩ = 84

Words and Music by
VAN MORRISON

Intro:

Into the Mystic - 4 - 1

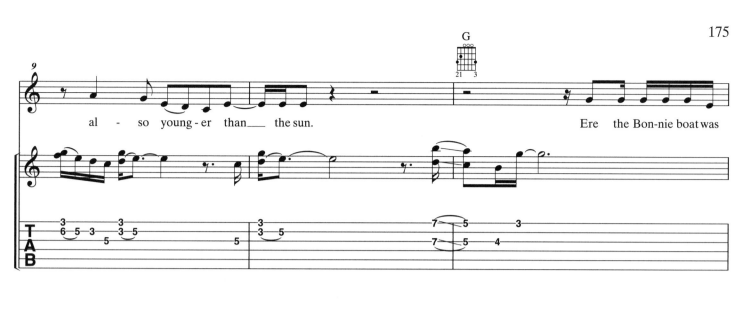

al - so young-er than___ the sun.   Ere the Bon-nie boat was

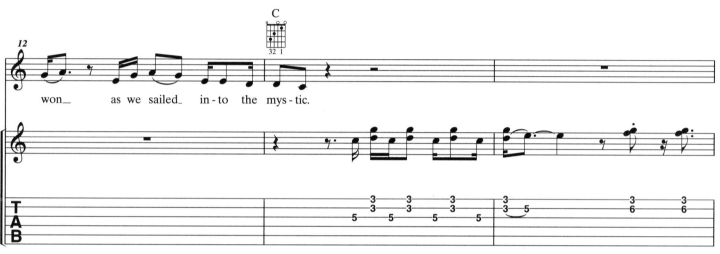

won___   as we sailed__ in-to the mys - tic.

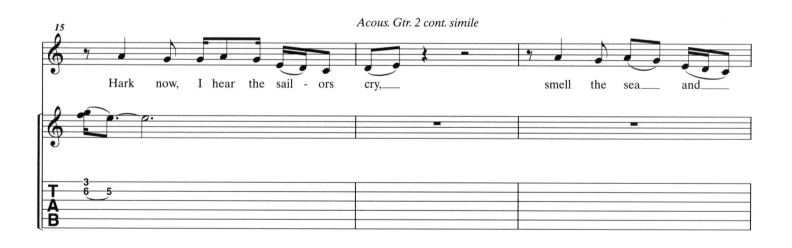

Acous. Gtr. 2 cont. simile

Hark   now, I hear the sail - ors   cry,___   smell the sea___ and___

feel the sky.___   Let your soul   and   spir-its fly_____ in-to the mys - tic.___

KASHMIR

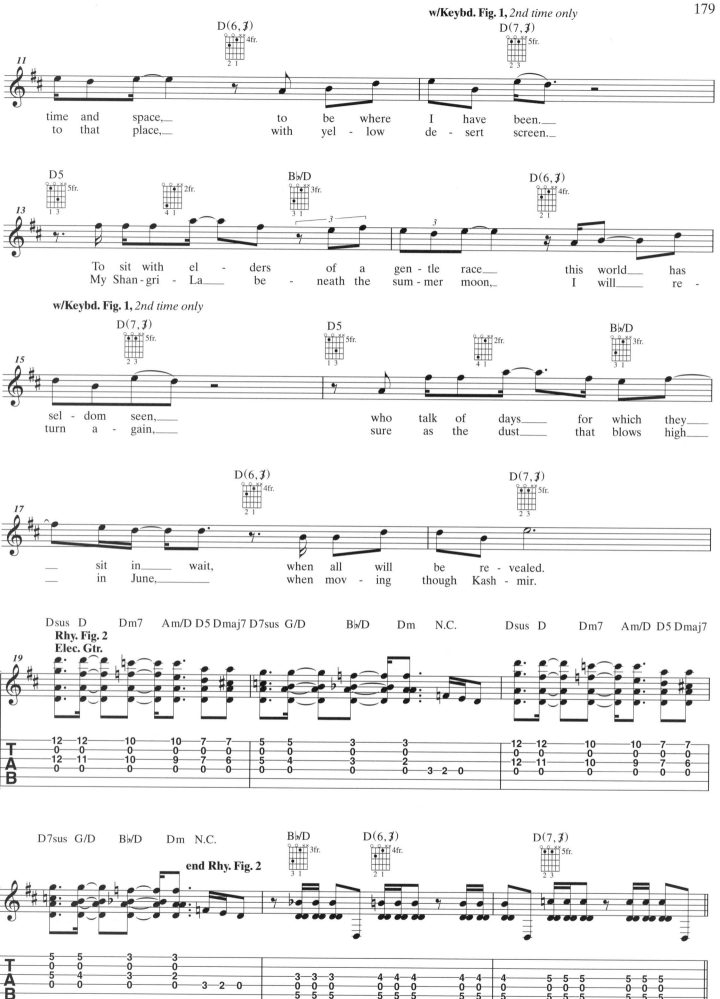

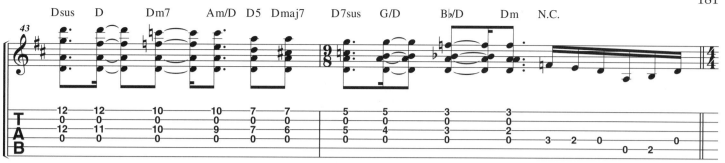

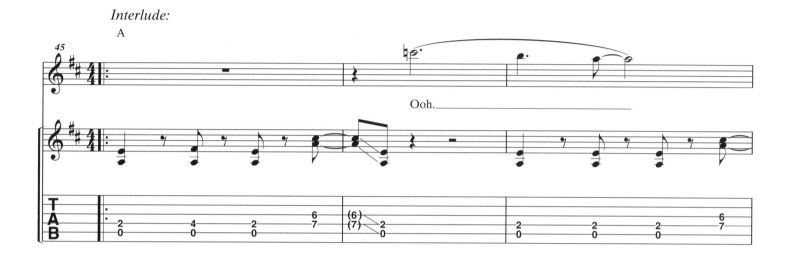

Interlude:

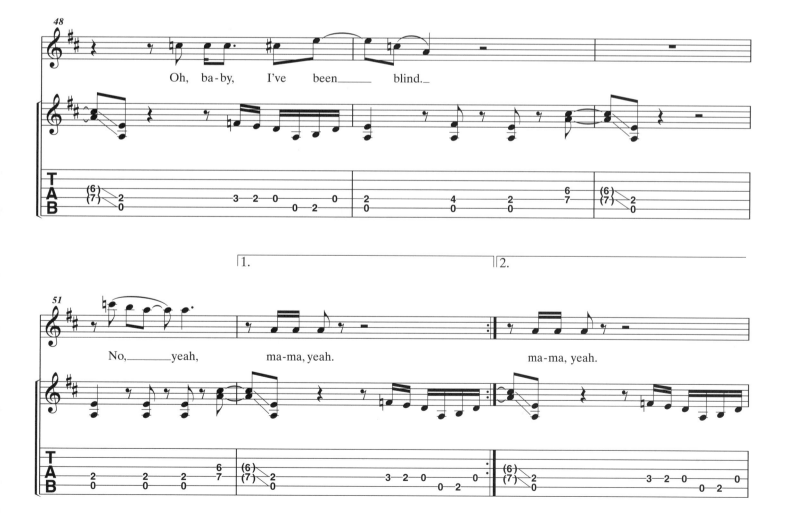

KNOCKING ON HEAVEN'S DOOR

Moderately slow ♩ = 70

Words and Music by
BOB DYLAN

Knocking on Heaven's Door - 2 - 1

LAYLA

Words and Music by
ERIC CLAPTON and JIM GORDON

Moderately ♩ = 117

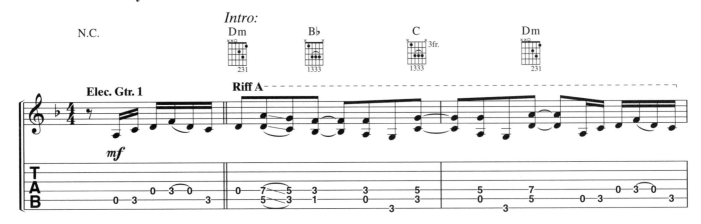

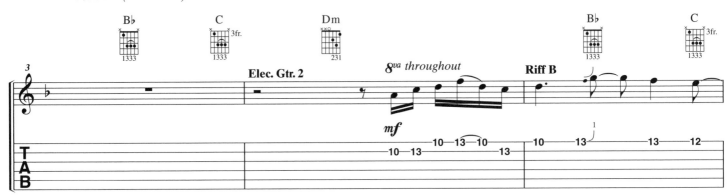

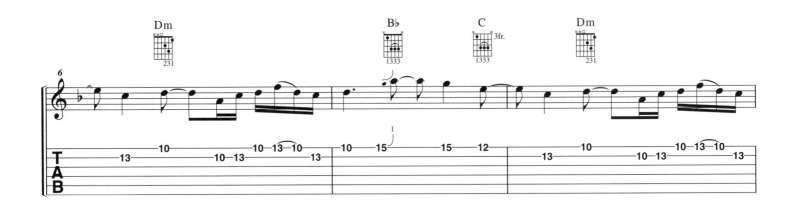

Layla - 6 - 1

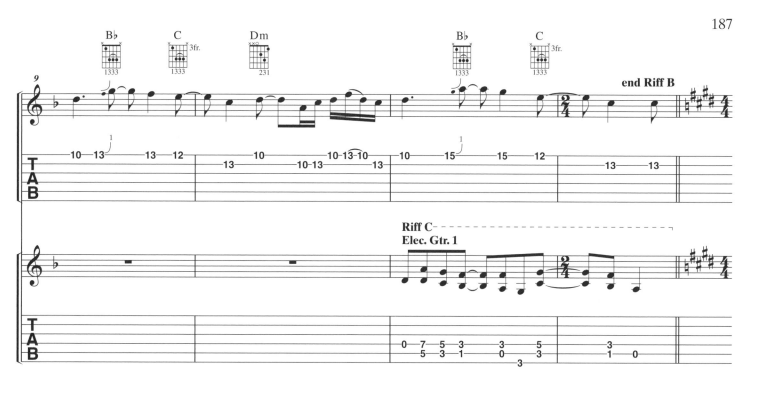

𝄋 *Verse:*

Elec. Gtr. 1 tacet.

Elec. Gtr. 1

Cont. rhy. simile

1. (A) what - 'll you do____ when you get lone - ly,____
2. I tried to give you____ con - so - la - tion____
3. So, make the best of____ the sit - u - a - tion,____

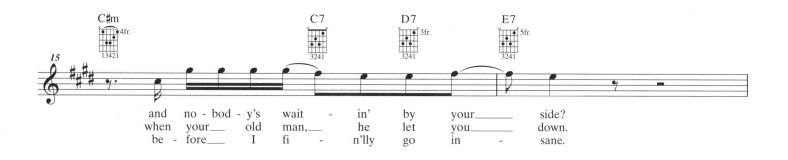

and no - bod - y's wait - in' by your_____ side?
when your___ old man,___ he let you_____ down.
be - fore___ I fi - n'lly go in - sane.

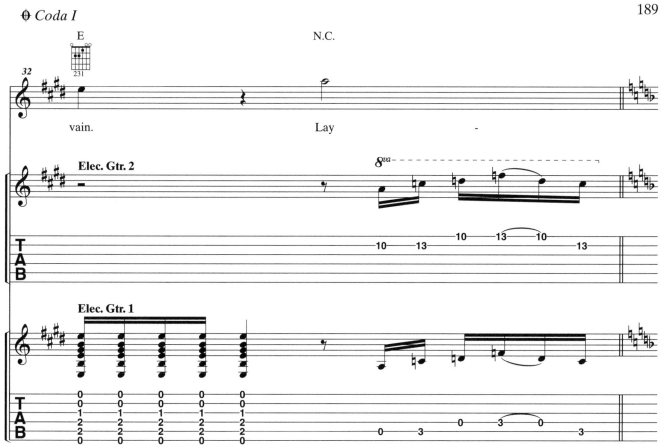

⊕ *Coda I*

vain.　　　　　　　Lay -

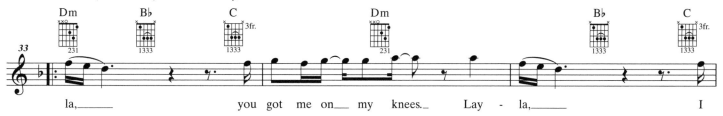

Chorus:

w/Riff A *(Elec. Gtr. 1) 4 times*
w/Riff B *(Elec. Gtr. 2) 1st 4 meas. only, 2 times*

la,＿＿＿　　　　you got me on＿ my knees.＿　Lay - la,＿＿＿　　　　I

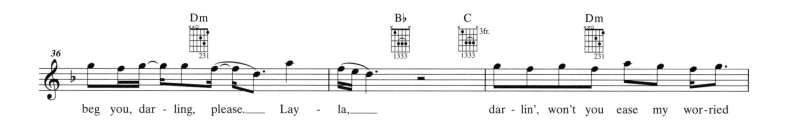

beg you, dar - ling, please.＿ Lay - la,＿＿＿　　　　　dar - lin', won't you ease my wor-ried

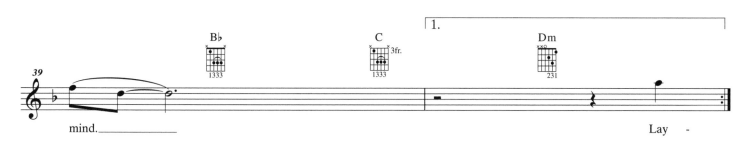

mind.＿＿＿　　　　　　　　　　　　　　　　　　　　　　　　　　　Lay -

LIKE A PRAYER

Words and Music by
MADONNA CICCONE
and PAT LEONARD

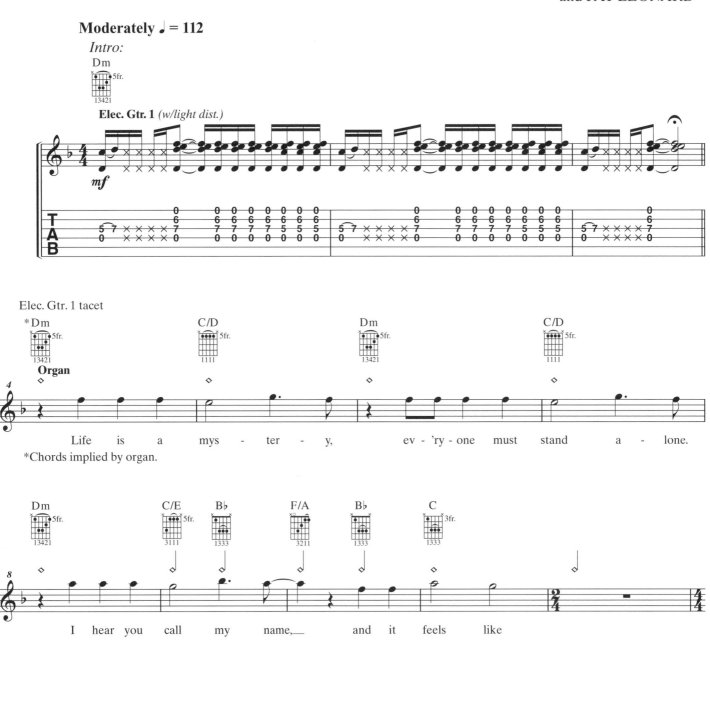

Life is a mys-ter-y, ev-'ry-one must stand a - lone.

*Chords implied by organ.

I hear you call my name,___ and it feels like

home.___

Like a Prayer - 6 - 1

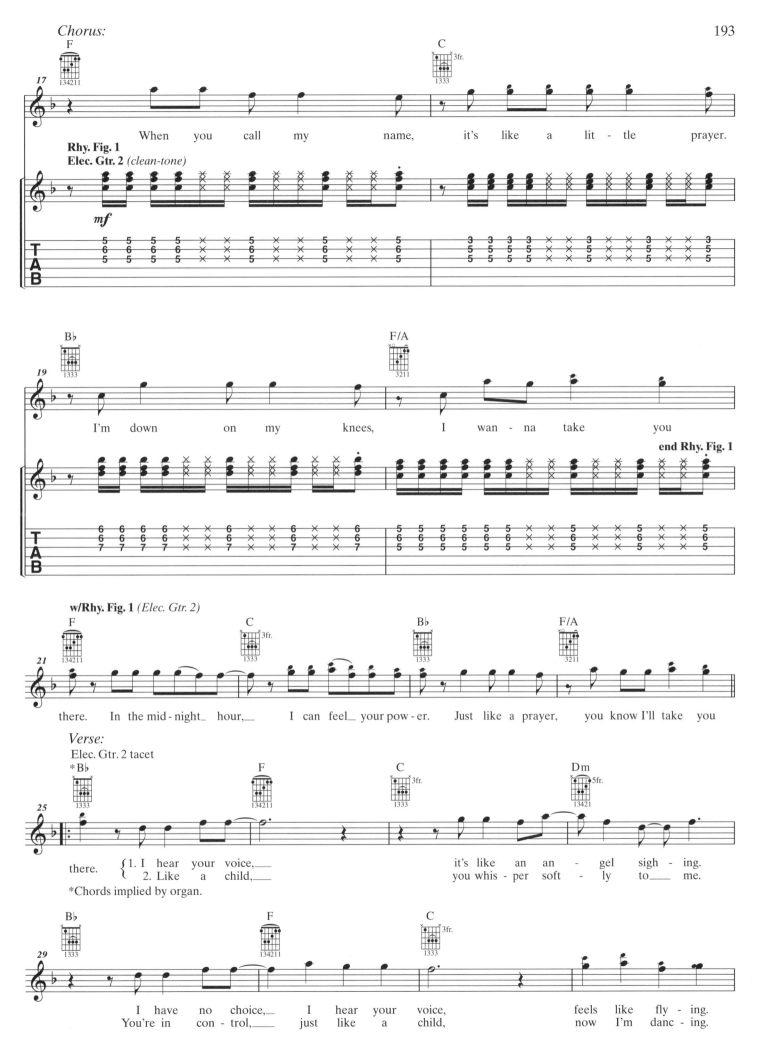

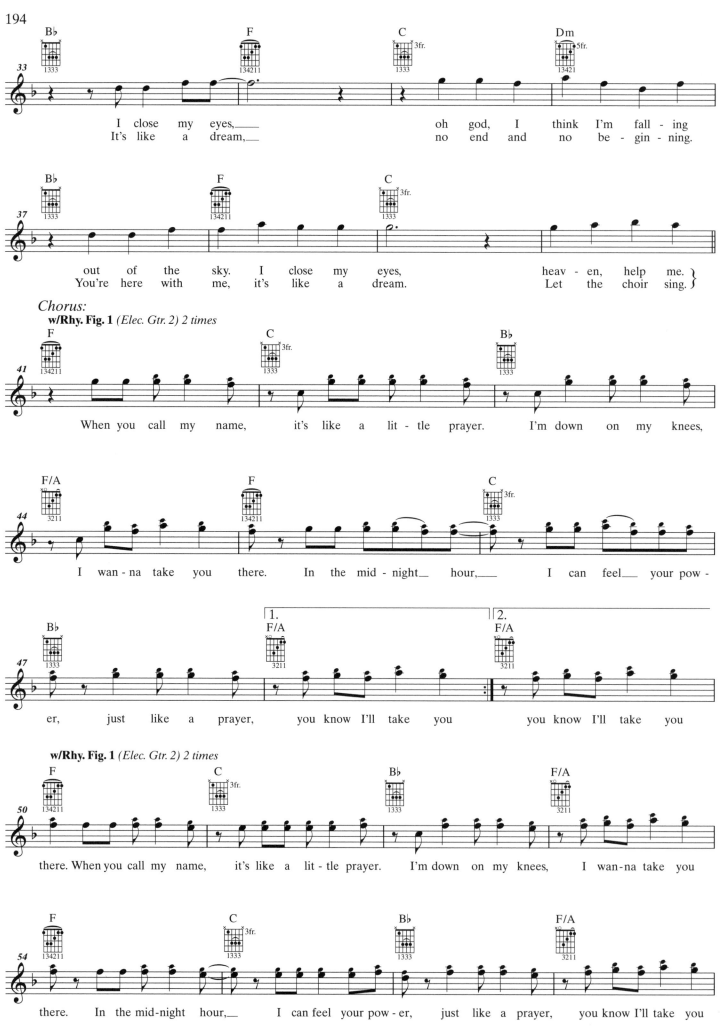

Chorus:

Like a Prayer - 6 - 3

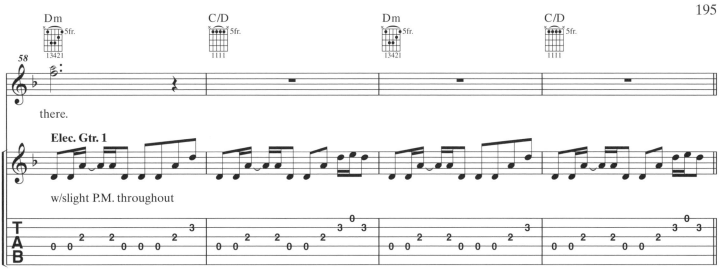

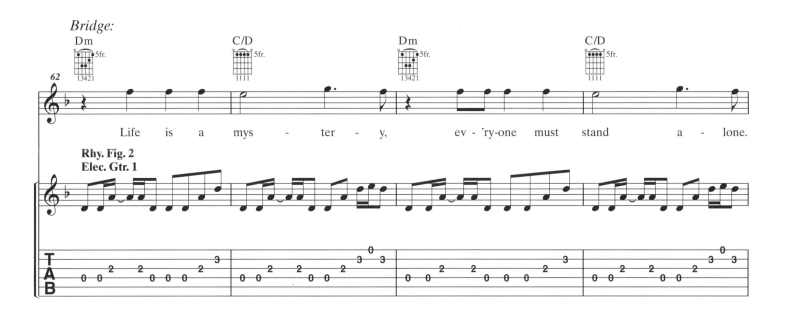

Bridge:

Life is a mys - ter - y, ev - 'ry-one must stand a - lone.

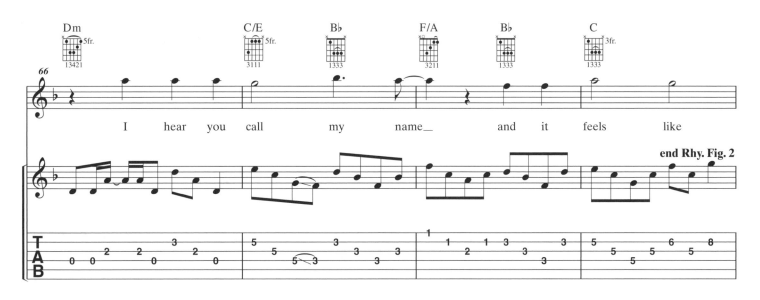

I hear you call my name__ and it feels like

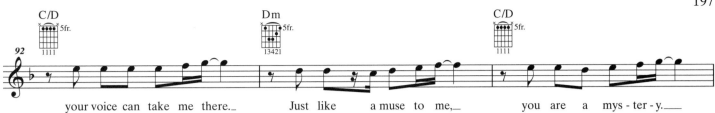

your voice can take me there.__ Just like a muse to me,__ you are a mys - ter - y.__

Just like a dream,__ you are not what you__ seem.__ Just like a prayer, no

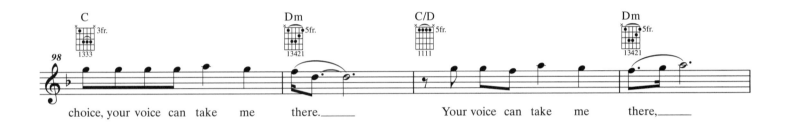

choice, your voice can take me there._____ Your voice can take me there,_____

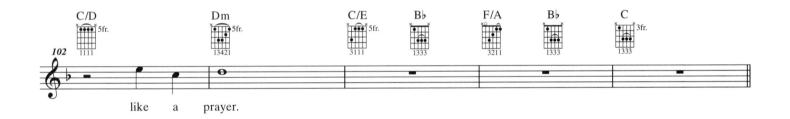

like a prayer.

Outro:
w/Rhy. Fig. 2 *(Elec. Gtr. 1)*

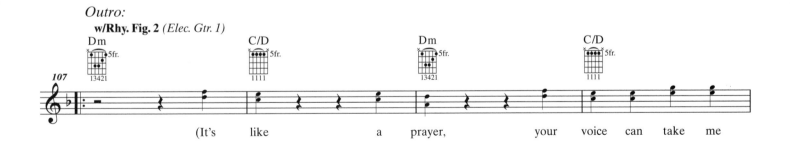

(It's like a prayer, your voice can take me

Repeat and fade

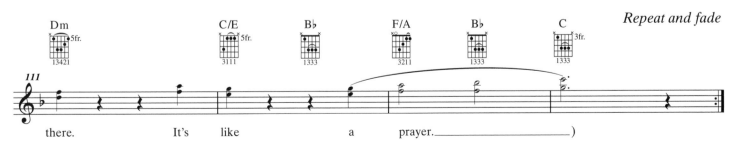

there. It's like a prayer._____)

LOLA

Words and Music by
RAY DAVIES

Lola - 4 - 1

Lola - 4 - 4

LONDON CALLING

Words and Music by
**JOE STRUMMER, MICK JONES,
PAUL SIMONON and TOPPER HEADON**

London Calling - 3 - 1

MOONDANCE

Words and Music by
VAN MORRISON

Moderately ♩ = 136

Intro:
Acous. Gtr.

1. Well, it's a

Verse:
Cont. rhy. simile

(1.4.) mar - vel - ous night___ for a moon - dance with___ the stars up a - bove in your eyes,
(2.) wan - na make love___ to you to - night, I___ can't wait 'til the morn - ing has come.
3. *Instrumental*

a fan - tab - u - lous night___ to make ro - mance 'neath the
And I know now the time_____ is just___ right and straight

cov - er of Oc - to - ber skies. And all the leaves on the trees are
in - to my arms___ you will run. And when you come, my heart will be

fall - ing to the sound of the breez - es that blow. And I'm
wait - ing to make sure that you're nev - er a - lone. There and

Moondance - 3 - 1

LOSING MY RELIGION

Words and Music by
WILLIAM BERRY, PETER BUCK,
MICHAEL MILLS and MICHAEL STIPE

Moderately ♩ = 126

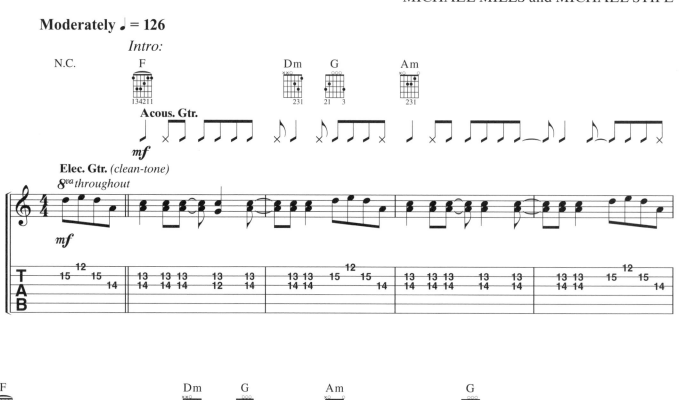

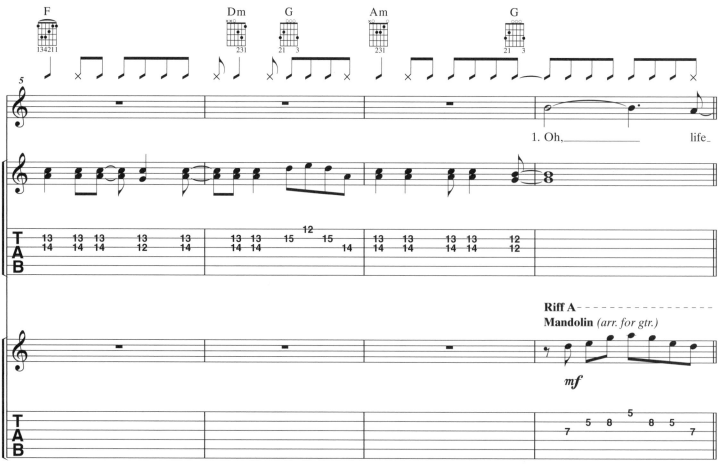

Losing My Religion - 6 - 1

Verse:

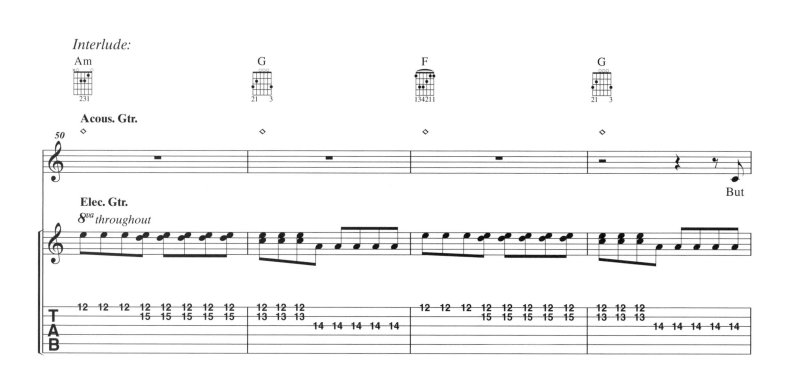

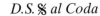

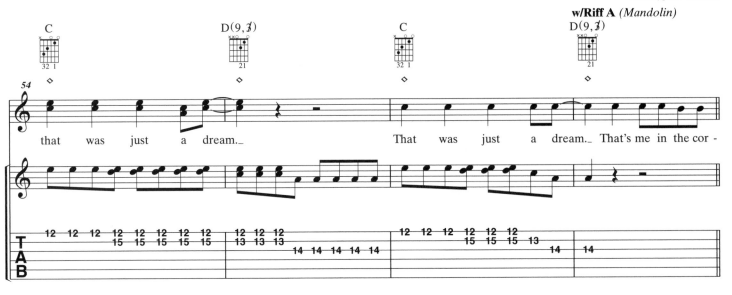

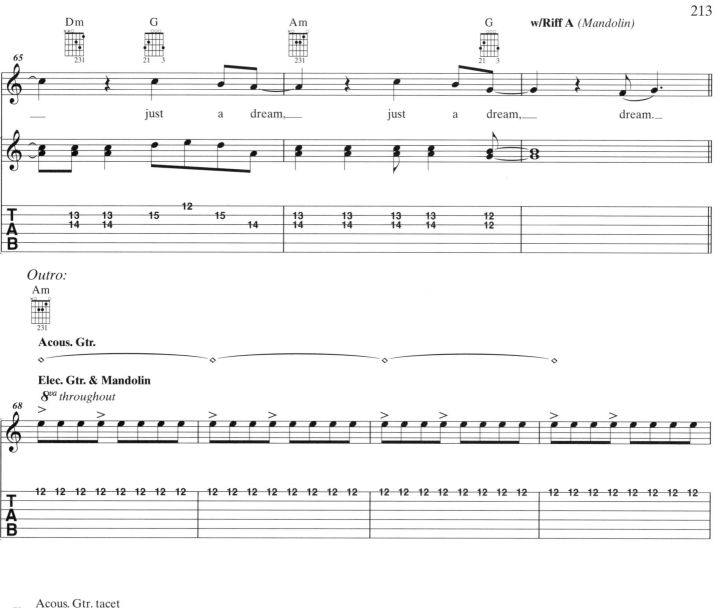

Outro:

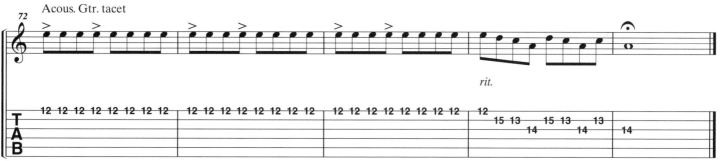

Verse 2:
Every whisper of every hour
I'm choosing my confession, trying to keep an eye on you,
Like a hurt lost and blinded fool, fool.
Oh no, I've said too much, I set it up.
Consider this; consider this, the hint of the century; consider this.
The slip that brought me to my knees failed.
What if all these fantasies come flailing around?
Now I've said too much.
(To Chorus:)

LUST FOR LIFE

Words and Music by
DAVID BOWIE and IGGY POP

Lust for Life - 6 - 1

Lust for Life - 6 - 2

1. Here___ comes John - ny Yen___ a - gain with the
2.3. *See additional lyrics*

li - quor and drugs, and a flesh ma - chine.

He's gon - na do an - oth - er strip - tease.

Hey, man, where'd you get___ that lo - tion?

I've been___ hurt - ing since I bought the gim - mick 'bout

some-thing called love, yeah, some-thing called love. Well,

that's like hyp - no - tiz - ing chick - ens.

Chorus:

Well, I'm just___ a mod - ern guy.___

Of course, I've had it in___ my ear be - fore.___ 'Cause of a

lust for life.

I've got a

Fade out

lust for life.

Chorus:

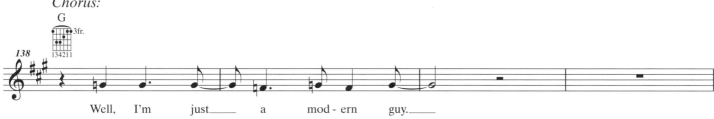

Well, I'm just___ a mod-ern guy.___

Of course, I've had it in___ my ear be-fore.___ 'Cause of a

lust for life.

'Cause of a

D.S. % and fade

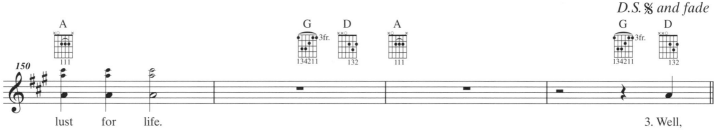

lust for life.

3. Well,

Verse 2:
I'm worth a million in prizes,
With my torture film.
Drive a G.T.O.,
Wear a uniform,
All on government loan.

I'm worth a million in prizes,
Yeah, I'm through with sleeping on the sidewalk.
No more beating my brains,
No more beating my brains,
With the liquor and drugs,
With the liquor and drugs.
(To Chorus:)

Verse 3:
Well, here comes Johnny Yen again
With the liquor and drugs,
And a flesh machine.
I know he's gonna do another striptease.

Hey, man, where'd ya get that lotion?
Your skin starts itching once you buy the gimmick
About something called love.
Oh, love, love, love.
Well, that's like hypnotizing chickens.
(To Chorus:)

MAGGIE MAY

Words and Music by
ROD STEWART and MARTIN QUITTENTON

Maggie May - 4 - 1

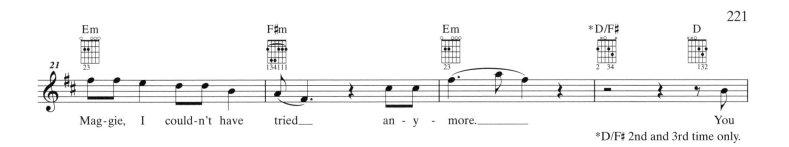

Mag-gie, I could-n't have tried___ an - y - more._____ You

*D/F♯ 2nd and 3rd time only.

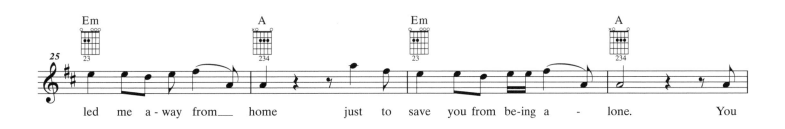

led me a-way from___ home just to save you from be-ing a - lone. You

To Coda ⊕ | 1.2. | | 3. |

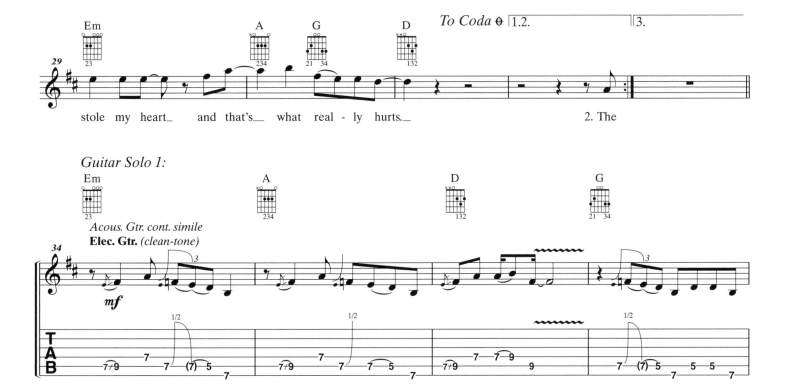

stole my heart_ and that's___ what real - ly hurts.___ 2. The

Guitar Solo 1:

Acous. Gtr. cont. simile
Elec. Gtr. *(clean-tone)*

mf

D.S. 𝄋 *al Coda*

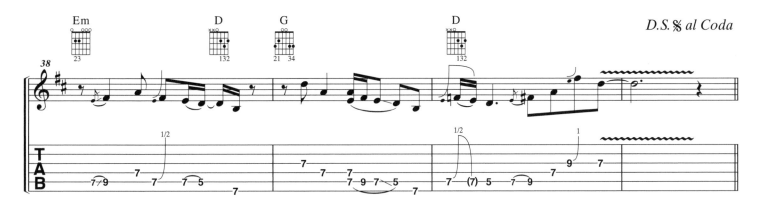

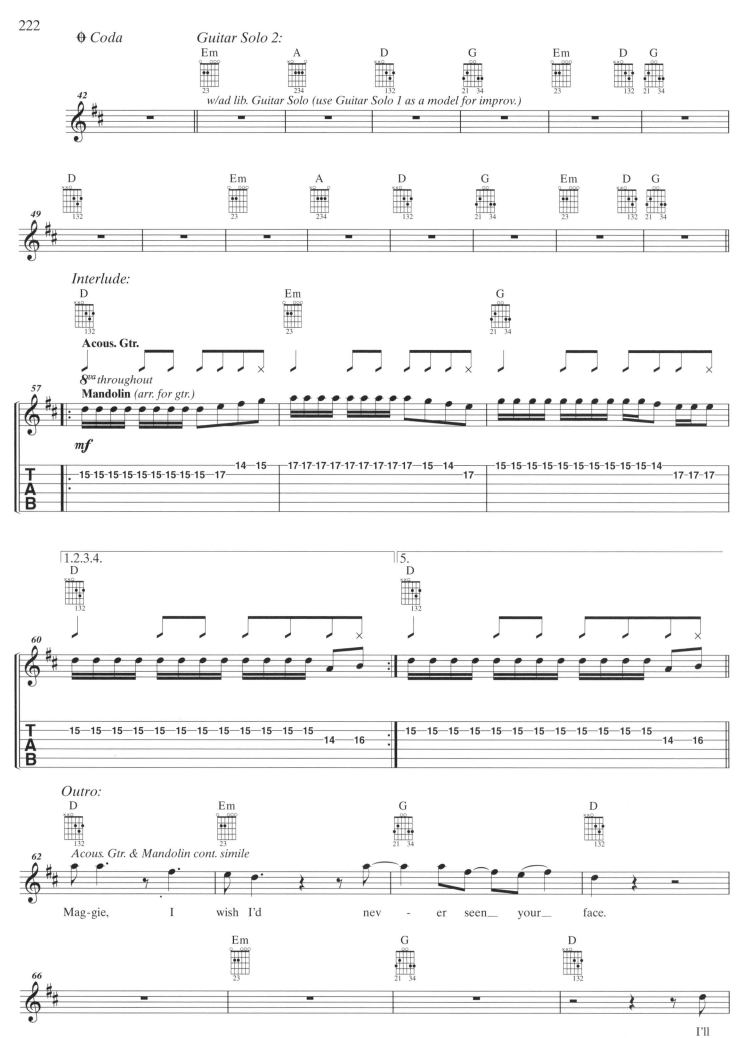

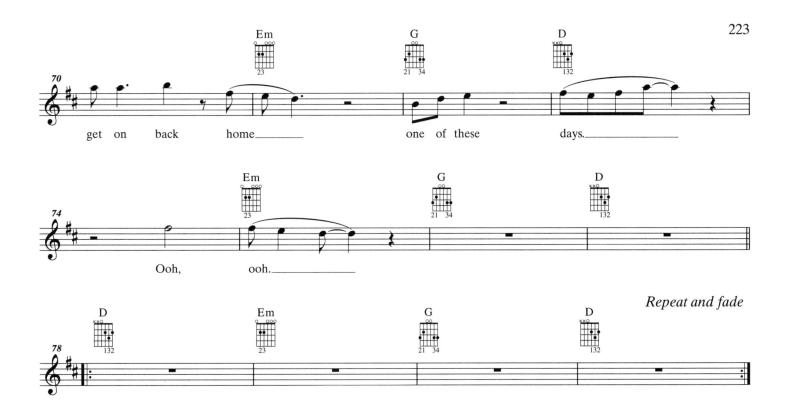

Repeat and fade

Verse 2:
The morning sun, when it's in your face,
Really shows your age.
But that don't worry me none,
In my eyes you're everything.
I laughed at all of your jokes,
My love you didn't need to coax.
Oh, Maggie, I couldn't have tried anymore.
You lead me away from home
Just to save you from being alone.
You stole my soul and that's a
Pain I can do without.

Verse 3:
All I needed was a friend
To lend a guiding hand.
But you turned into a lover and, mother,
What a lover, you wore me out.
All you did was wreck my bed,
And in the morning kick me in the head.
Oh, Maggie, I couldn't have tried anymore.
You lead me away from home
'Cause you didn't want to be alone.
You stole my heart,
I couldn't leave you if I tried.
(To Guitar Solo 1:)

Verse 4:
I suppose I could collect my books
And get on back to school.
Or steal my daddy's cue,
And make a living out of playing pool.
Or find myself a rock and roll band
That needs a helping hand.
Oh, Maggie, I wish I'd never seen your face.
You made a first-class fool out of me,
But I'm as blind as a fool can be.
You stole my heart
But I love you anyway.
(To Guitar Solo 2:)

NO WOMAN, NO CRY

Words and Music by
VINCENT FORD

No Woman, No Cry - 3 - 1

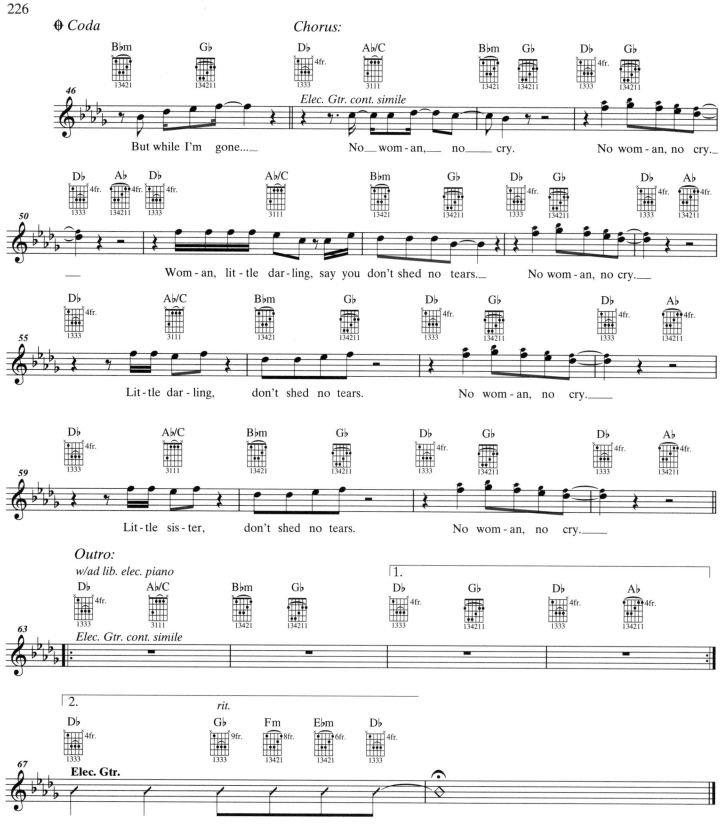

Verses 2 & 3:
I remember when we used to sit
In the government yard in Trenchtown.
And then Georgie would make the fire light,
As it was logwood burnin' through the night.
Then we would cook cornmeal porridge,
Of which I'll share with you.
My feet is my only carriage,
So I've got to push on through.
But, while I'm gone I mean...
(1st time to Bridge:)
(2nd time to Chorus:)

PARADISE CITY

To match record key, tune down a 1/2 step

Words and Music by
STEVEN ADLER, SAUL HUDSON,
DUFF MCKAGAN, W. AXL ROSE
and IZZY STRADLIN

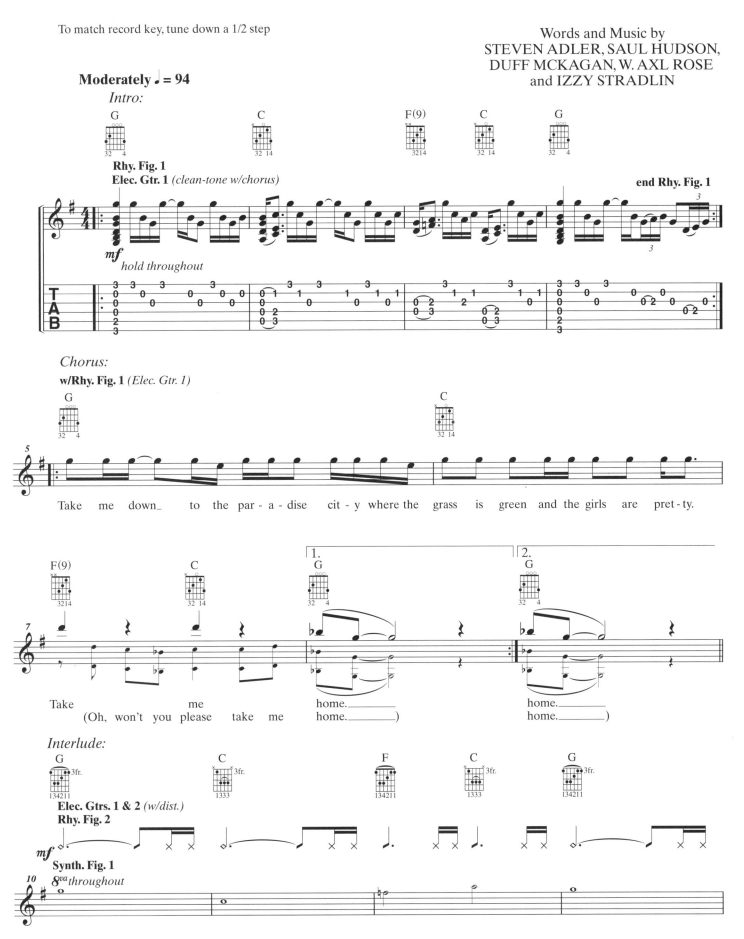

Paradise City - 9 - 1

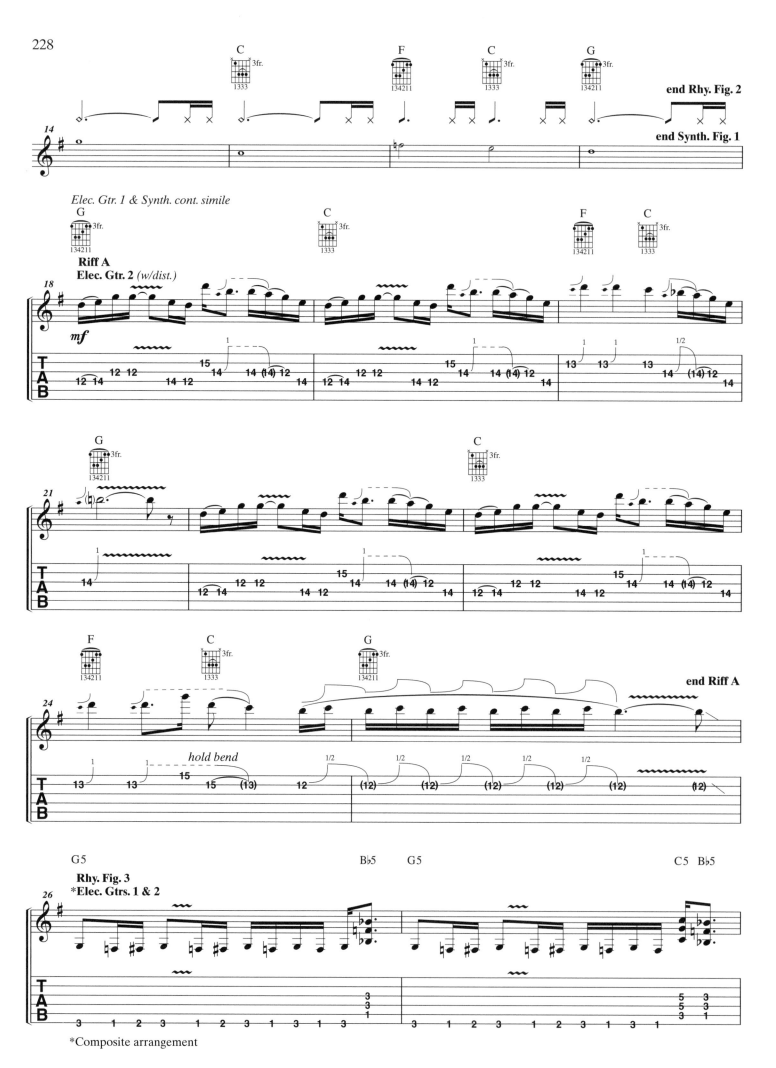

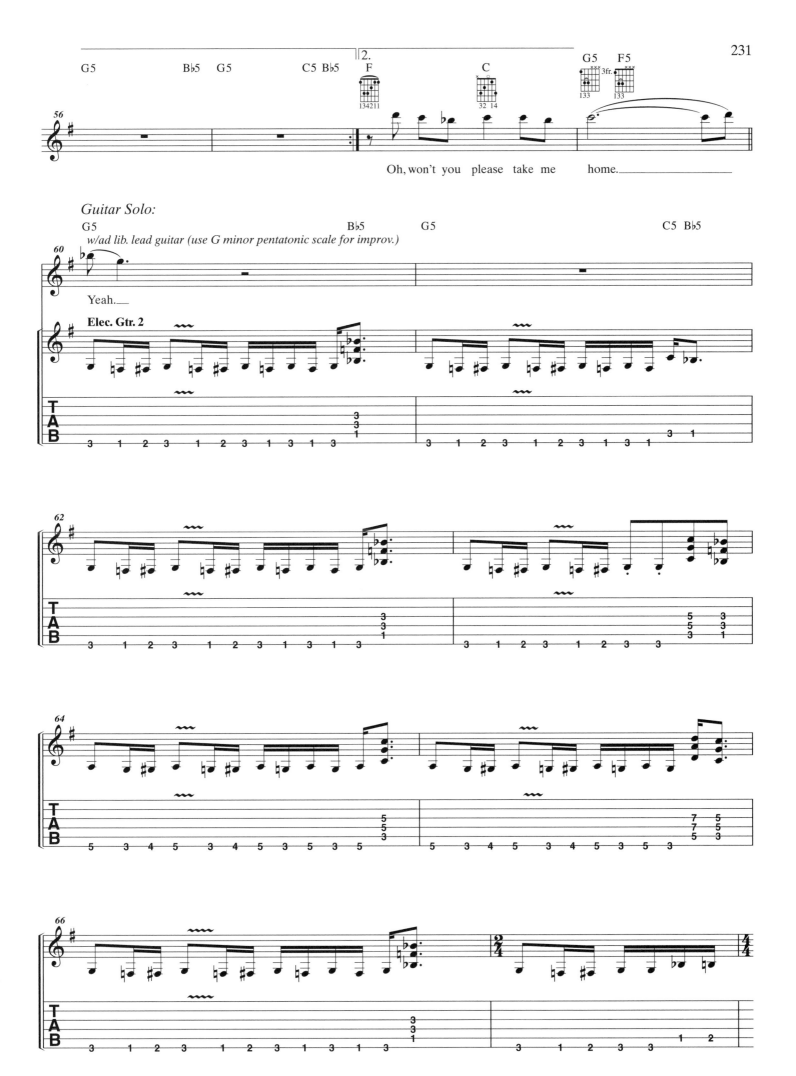

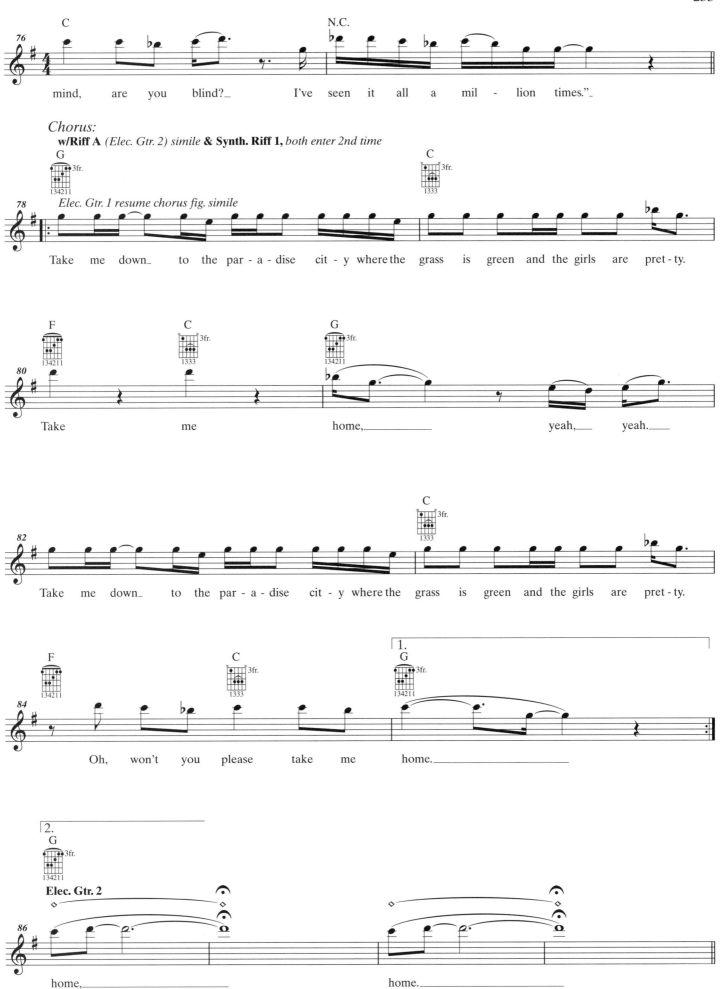

Chorus:
w/Riff A *(Elec. Gtr. 2) simile* **& Synth. Riff 1,** *both enter 2nd time*

1.2. Take me down_ to the par - a - dise cit - y where the grass is green and the girls are pret - ty.__

3.–7. *See additional lyrics*

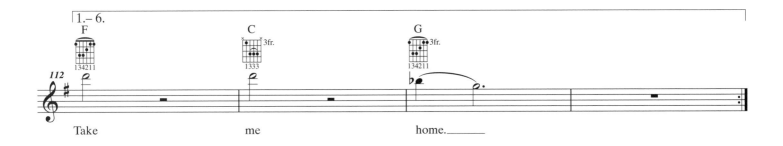

Take me home._____

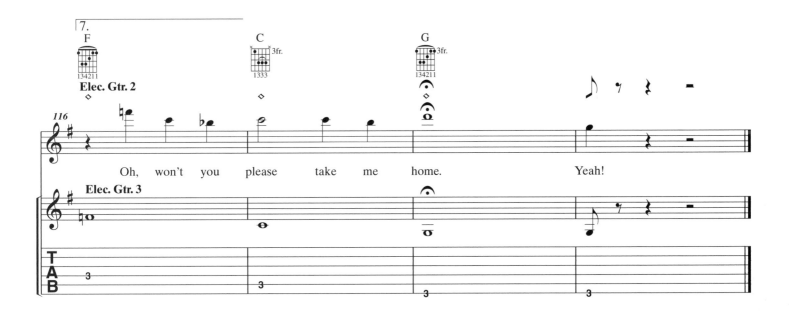

Oh, won't you please take me home. Yeah!

Outro additional lyrics:
Take me down to the paradise city
Where the grass is green and the girls are pretty.
Oh, won't you please take me home.
Take me down, take me 'round.
Oh, won't you please take me home.
I wanna see how good you can be.
Oh, won't you please take me home.
I wanna see how good you can be.
Oh, won't you please take me home.
Take me down to the paradise city
Where the grass is green and the girls are pretty.
Oh, won't you please take me home.
I wanna know, I wanna know.

PARANOID

Words and Music by
FRANK IOMMI, JOHN OSBOURNE,
WILLIAM WARD and TERENCE BUTLER

Moderately fast ♩ = 156

Intro:
Band enter 3rd time

Play 4 times

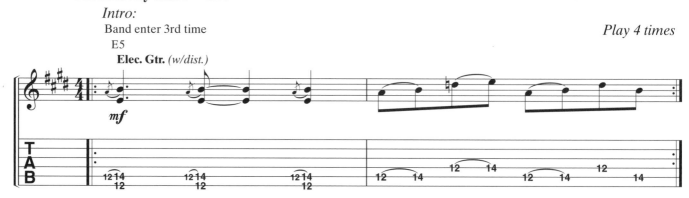

% *Verses 1 & 4:*

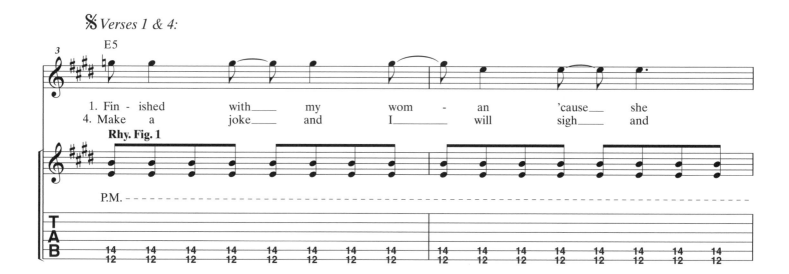

1. Fin - ished with___ my wom - an 'cause___ she
4. Make a joke___ and I___ will sigh___ and

could - n't help___ me with my mind. Peo - ple think___ I'm in -
you will laugh___ and I will cry. Hap - pi - ness___ I can -

Paranoid - 4 - 1

Interlude:

Verse 3:

I need some-one to___ show me___ the things in life___ that I can't find.

I can't see___ the things___ that make___ true hap - pi - ness,___ I must be blind.

Guitar Solo:

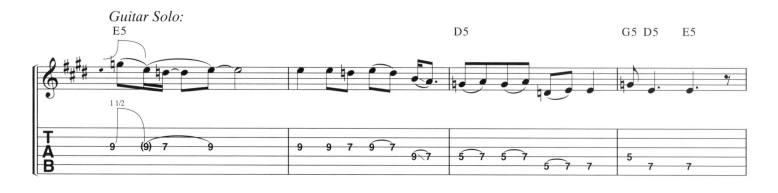

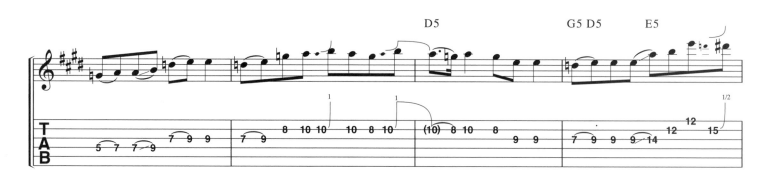

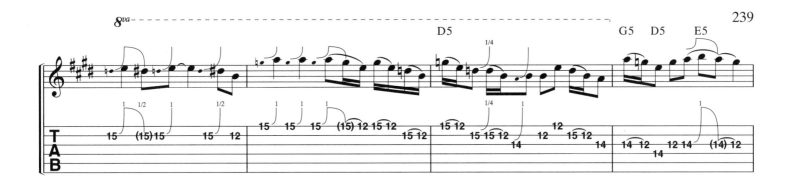

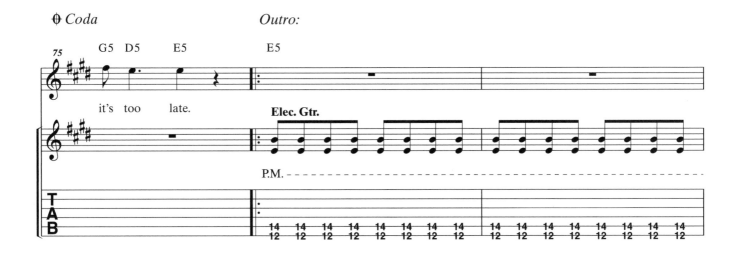

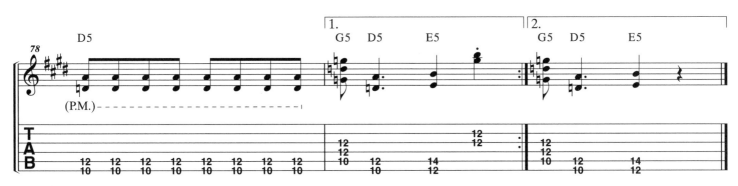

Paranoid - 4 - 4

PARANOID ANDROID

Words and Music by
THOMAS YORKE, EDWARD O'BRIEN,
COLIN GREENWOOD, JONATHAN GREENWOOD
and PHILIP SELWAY

Verses 1 & 2:

w/Rhy. Fig. 1 *(Acous. Gtr.) simile*

1. Please, could you stop the noise I'm try'n' to get some rest,
2. When I am king you will be first a-gainst the wall,

Elec. Gtr. 1

w/Rhy. Fig. 1 *(Acous. Gtr.) 1st 4 meas. only, simile*

from all the un-born chick-en voic-es in my head.
with your o-pin-ion which is of no con-se-quence at

Chorus:

244

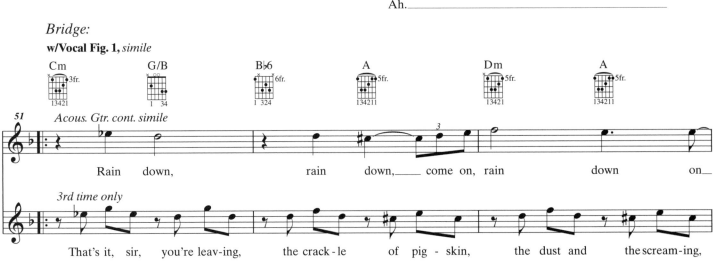

(What's So Funny 'Bout)
PEACE LOVE AND UNDERSTANDING?

Words and Music by
NICK LOWE

Moderately fast ♩ = 140

*Bass plays G

Cont. in slashes

(What's So Funny 'bout) Peace Love and Understanding? - 2 - 1

(What's So Funny 'bout) Peace Love and Understanding? - 2 - 2

PERSONALITY CRISIS

Bright rock ♩ = 152

Words and Music by
DAVID JOHANSEN and JOHNNY THUNDERS

Verse 1:

Verse 4:
Now, with all the trust and faith that Mother Nature sends,
Your mirror's getting jammed up with all your friends.
That's personality, everything is starting to blend. (You thought you'd won.)
Personality, when your mind starts to blend.
Got so much personality, passion of a friend of a friend of a friend of a friend.
(To Coda)

RADIO FREE EUROPE

Words and Music by
WILLIAM BERRY, PETER BUCK,
MICHAEL MILLS and MICHAEL STIPE

(DON'T FEAR) THE REAPER

Words and Music by
DONALD ROESER

*Composite arrangement.

All our times have come.

Here but now they're gone.

Sea-sons don't fear the reap - er, nor do the wind, the sun, or the rain.

Come on, ba - by.

We can be like they are. Don't fear the reap-

Chorus:

w/Rhy. Fig. 1 *(Elec. Gtr. 1) 5 times*

w/ad lib. gtr. fills (use Am scale for improvising)

Interlude:

w/Rhy. Fig. 1 *(Elec. Gtr. 1) 4 times*

Verse 2:

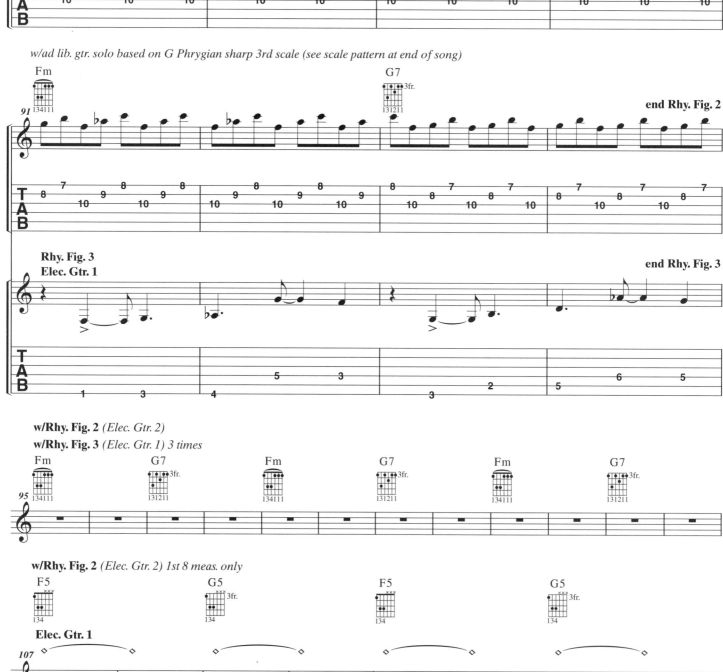

262

w/ad lib. gtr. solo based on G Phrygian sharp 3rd scale (see scale pattern at end of song)

end Rhy. Fig. 2

Rhy. Fig. 3
Elec. Gtr. 1

end Rhy. Fig. 3

w/Rhy. Fig. 2 *(Elec. Gtr. 2)*
w/Rhy. Fig. 3 *(Elec. Gtr. 1) 3 times*

w/Rhy. Fig. 2 *(Elec. Gtr. 2) 1st 8 meas. only*

Elec. Gtr. 1

Interlude:
w/Rhy. Fig. 1 *(Elec. Gtr. 1) 4 times*

Verse 3:

STAYIN' ALIVE

Words and Music by
BARRY GIBB, MAURICE GIBB
and ROBIN GIBB

*Composite arrangement.

Stayin' Alive - 3 - 1

Stayin' Alive - 3 - 2

RESPECT

Words and Music by
OTIS REDDING

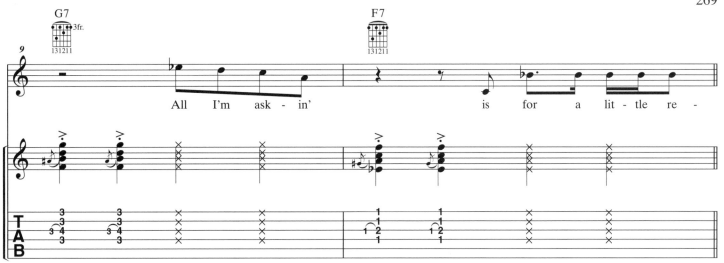

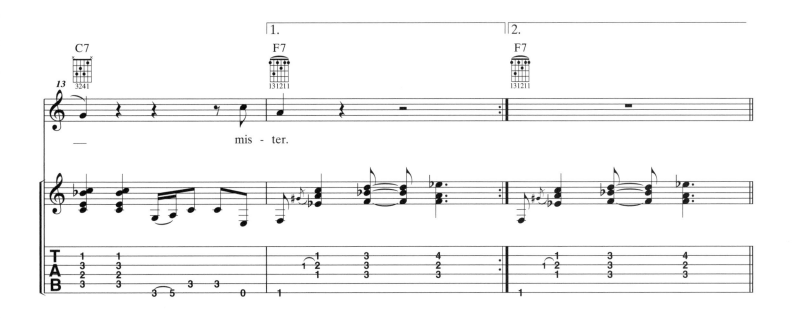

Chorus:

SHEENA IS A PUNK ROCKER

Words and Music by
JEFFREY HYMAN, JOHN CUMMINGS,
DOUGLAS COLVIN and THOMAS ERDELYI

SHOULD I STAY OR SHOULD I GO

Words and Music by
JOE STRUMMER and MICK JONES

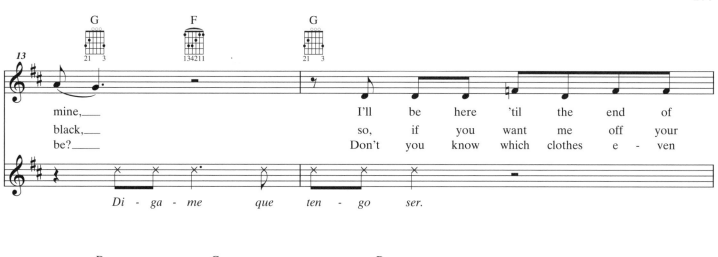

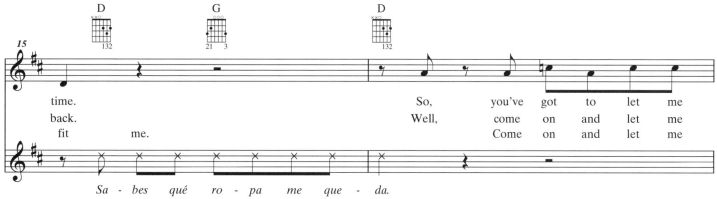

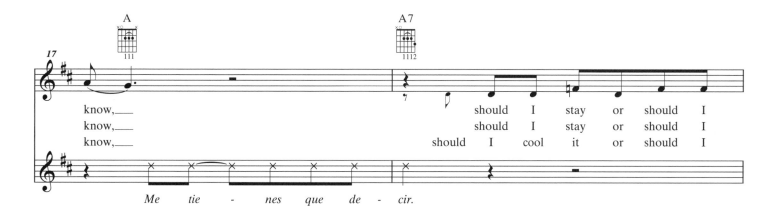

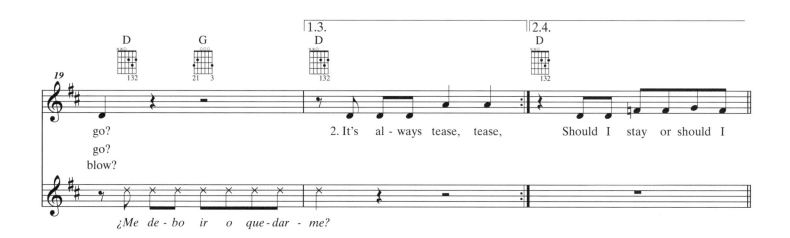

SPIRIT IN THE SKY

Words and Music by
NORMAN GREENBAUM

Acous. Gtr. enters 3rd time.

1. When I die and they lay me to rest,___ gon-na go___ to the place___ that's the best.

2.3. *See additional lyrics*

When I lay me down___ to die, go-in' up___ to the spir - it in the sky.

Go-in' up___ to the spir - it in the sky,___ that's where I'm gon-na go___ when I die.___

Spirit in the Sky - 4 - 1

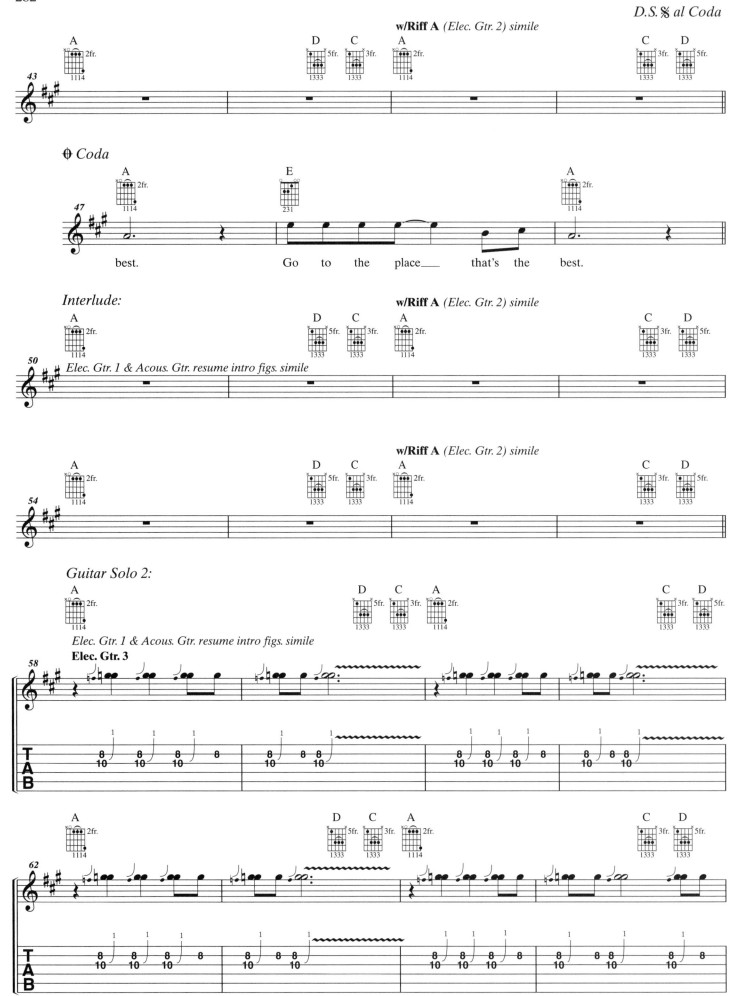

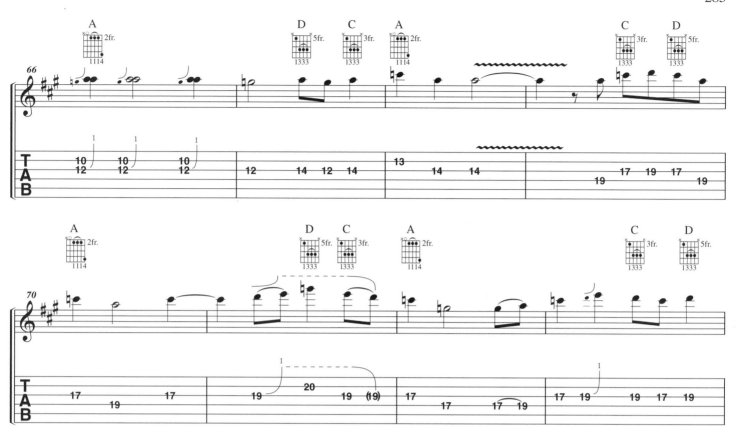

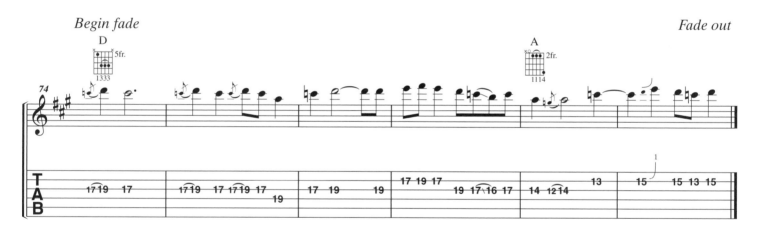

Verse 2:
Prepare yourself, you know it's a must,
Gotta have a friend in Jesus.
So you know that when you die,
He's gonna recommend you to the spirit in the sky.
Gonna recommend you to the spirit in the sky,
That's where you're gonna go when you die.
When you die and they lay you to rest,
You're gonna go to the place that's the best.

Verse 3:
Never been a sinner, I never sinned,
I got a friend in Jesus.
So you know that when I die,
He's gonna set me up with the spirit in the sky.
Oh, set me up with the spirit in the sky,
That's where I'm gonna go when I die.
When I die and they lay me to rest,
I'm gonna go to the place that's the best.
Go to the place that's the best.

STAIRWAY TO HEAVEN

*Slowly ♩ = 72

Words and Music by
JIMMY PAGE and ROBERT PLANT

*Gradual accelerando between tempos throughout the song.

There's a

Verse 1:

there's still time to change the road you're on.
your stair - way lies on the whis - p'rin' wind.

w/Rhy. Fig. 1 *(Elec. Gtr. 1 & Acous. Gtr.)*

And it makes me won - der,

Acous. Gtr. & Elec. Gtr. 1

ahh.

Interlude: ♩ = 90

Acous. Gtr. & Elec. Gtr. 1

hold throughout

Cont. in slashes

Guitar Solo: ♩ = 96

Acous. Gtr. & Elec. Gtr. 1

Cont. rhy. simile

Elec. Gtr. 2

mf

to be a rock___ and not to roll.___

And she's buy - ing a stair - way___ to heav - en.___

SWEET CHILD O' MINE

To match record key, tune down ½ step:

⑥ = E♭   ③ = G♭
⑤ = A♭   ② = B♭
④ = D♭   ① = E♭

Words and Music by
W. AXL ROSE, SLASH, IZZY STRADLIN,
DUFF McKAGAN and STEVEN ADLER

Moderately ♩ = 120

Intro:

Sweet Child O' Mine - 5 - 1

WALK ON THE WILD SIDE

Words and Music by
LOU REED

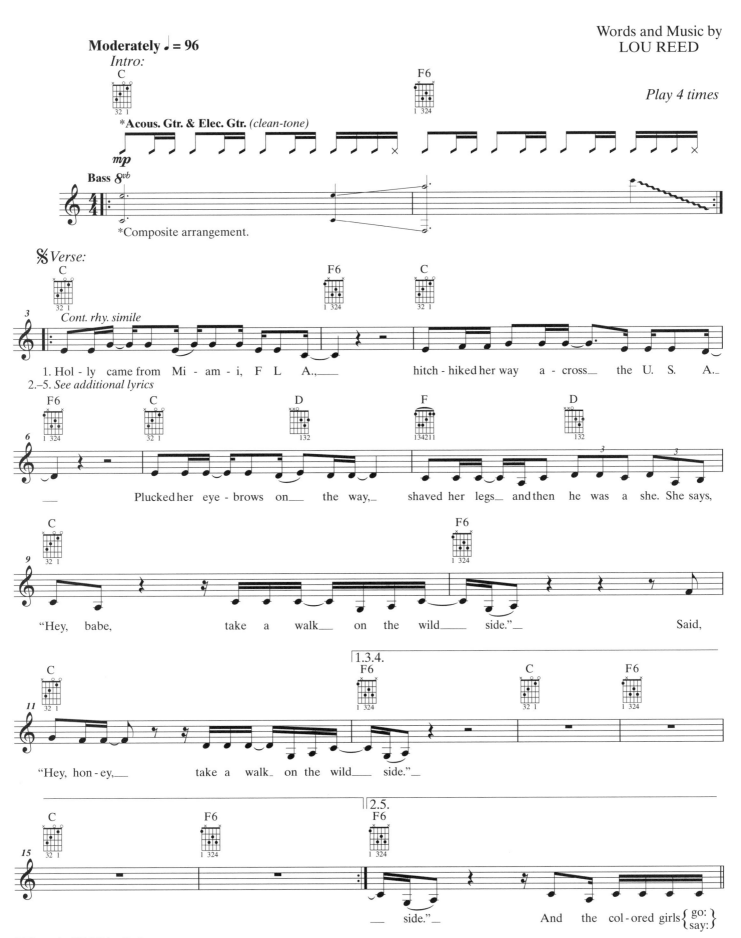

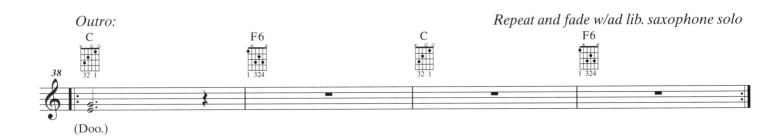

Outro: *Repeat and fade w/ad lib. saxophone solo*

(Doo.)

Verse 2:
Candy came from out on the island,
In the backroom, she was everybody's darling.
But she never lost her head,
Even when she was givin' head.
She says, "Hey, babe, take a walk on the wild side."
Said, "Hey, babe, take a walk on the wild side."
(To Bridge:)

Verse 3:
Little Joe never once gave it away,
Everybody had to pay and pay.
A hustle here and a hustle there,
New York City is the place where they said,
"Hey, babe, take a walk on the wild side."
I said, "Hey, Joe, take a walk on the wild side."

Verse 4:
Sugar Plum Fairy came and hit the streets,
Lookin' for soul food and a place to eat.
Went to the Apollo,
You should have seen him go-go-go.
They said, "Hey, sugar, take a walk on the wild side."
I said, "Hey, babe, take a walk on the wild side."
All right, huh.

Verse 5:
Jackie is just speeding away,
Thought she was James Dean for a day.
Then I guess she had to crash,
Valium would have helped that dash.
She said, "Hey, babe, take a walk on the wild side."
I said, "Hey, honey, take a walk on the wild side."
(To Bridge:)

TANGLED UP IN BLUE

Words and Music by
BOB DYLAN

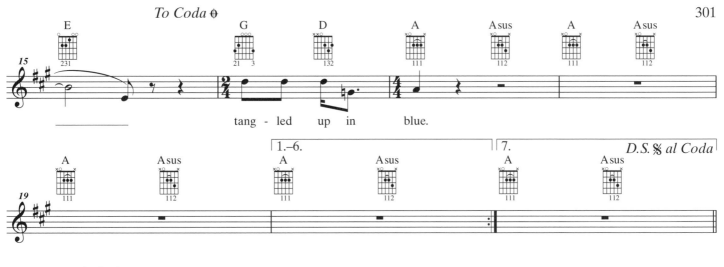

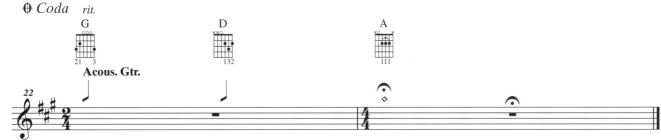

tang - led up in blue.

Verse 2:
She was married when we first met,
Soon to be divorced.
I helped her out of a jam, I guess,
But I used a little too much force.
We drove that car as far as we could,
Abandoned it out West.
Split up on a dark sad night
Both agreeing it was best.
She turned around to look at me
As I was walkin' away,
I heard her say over my shoulder,
"We'll meet again someday on the avenue,"
Tangled up in blue.

Verse 3:
I had a job in the great north woods
Working as a cook for a spell.
But I never did like it all that much
And one day the ax just fell.
So I drifted down to New Orleans
Where I happened to be employed,
Workin' for a while on a fishin' boat
Right outside of Delacroix.
But all the while I was alone
The past was close behind.
I seen a lot of women,
But she never escaped my mind, and I just grew,
Tangled up in blue.

Verse 4:
She was workin' in a topless place
And I stopped in for a beer.
I just kept lookin' at the side of her face
In the spotlight so clear.
And later on when the crowd thinned out
I's just about to do the same.
She was standing there in back of my chair,
Said to me, "Don't I know your name?"
I muttered somethin' underneath my breath,
She studied the lines on my face.
I must admit I felt a little uneasy
When she bent down to tie the laces of my shoe,
Tangled up in blue.

Verse 5:
She lit a burner on the stove
And offered me a pipe.
"I thought you'd never say hello," she said
"You look like the silent type."
Then she opened up a book of poems
And handed it to me,
Written by an Italian poet
From the thirteenth century.
And every one of them words rang true
And glowed like burnin' coal.
Pourin' off of every page
Like it was written in my soul from me to you,
Tangled up in blue.

Verse 6:
I lived with them on Montague Street
In a basement down the stairs,
There was music in the cafes at night
And revolution in the air.
Then he started into dealing with slaves
And something inside of him died.
She had to sell everything she owned
And froze up inside.
And when finally the bottom fell out
I became withdrawn,
The only thing I knew how to do
Was to keep on keepin' on like a bird that flew,
Tangled up in blue.

Verse 7:
So now I'm goin' back again,
I got to get to her somehow.
All the people we used to know
They're an illusion to me now.
Some are mathematicians,
Some are carpenter's wives.
Don't know how it all got started,
I don't know what they're doin' with their lives.
But me, I'm still on the road,
Headin' for another joint.
We always did feel the same,
We just saw it from a different point of view,
Tangled up in blue.

THANK YOU
(FALETTINME BE MICE ELF AGIN)

Words and Music by
SYLVESTER STEWART

Thank You (Falettinme Be Mice Elf Agin) - 2 - 2

THUNDER ROAD

Words and Music by
BRUCE SPRINGSTEEN

Thunder Road - 6 - 1

_ full of los-ers, I'm pull-ing out of here to win._____

Outro:

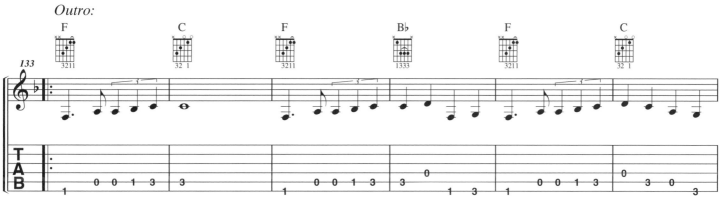

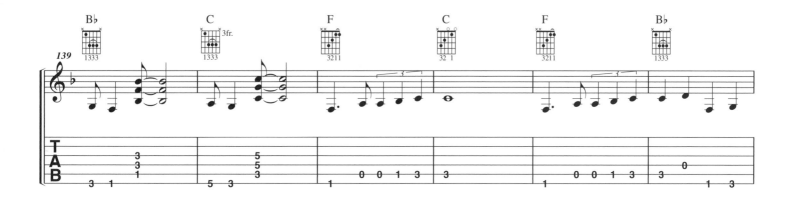

Repeat and fade

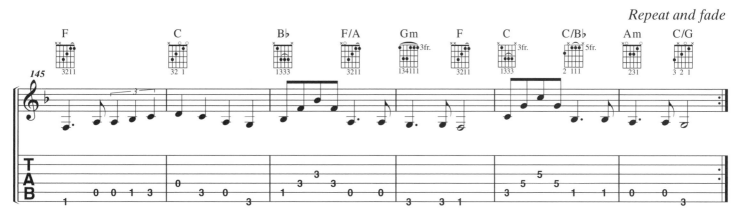

Thunder Road - 6 - 6

WELCOME TO THE JUNGLE

To match record key, tune down 1/2 step

Words and Music by
STEVEN ADLER, SAUL HUDSON,
DUFF MCKAGAN, W. AXL ROSE
and IZZY STRADLIN

Welcome to the Jungle - 7 - 1

312

⊕ *Coda*

Bridge:

Interlude:

Guitar Solo:

w/ad lib. gtr. solo (based on C#m pentatonic scale)

Verse 2:
Welcome to the jungle,
We take it day by day.
If you want it, you're gonna bleed,
But it's the price you pay.
And you're a very sexy girl
Who's very hard to please.
You can taste the bright lights,
But you won't get them for free.
In the jungle,
Welcome to the jungle.
Feel my, my, my, my serpentine.
Uh, ah. I wanna hear you scream!
(To Interlude:)

Verse 3:
Welcome to the jungle,
It gets worse here every day.
You learn to live like an animal
In the jungle where we play.
If you got a hunger for what you see,
You'll take it eventually.
You can have anything you want,
But you better not take it from me.
In the jungle,
Welcome to the jungle.
Watch it bring you to your
Sha na na na na na na na na na na na na
Knees, knees.
Uh. I'm gonna watch you bleed.
(To Bridge:)

WHAT'S GOING ON

Moderate R & B ♩ = 96

Words and Music by
MARVIN GAYE, AL CLEVELAND
and RENALDO BENSON

What's Going On - 3 - 1

WHIPPING POST

Words and Music by
GREGG ALLMAN

Tempo ♪ = 212

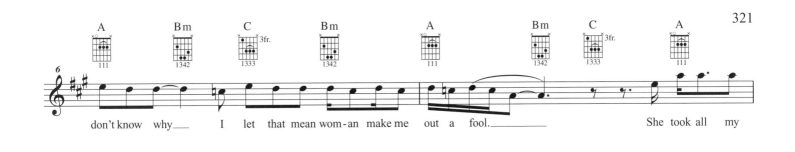

don't know why___ I let that mean wom-an make me out a fool.___ She took all my

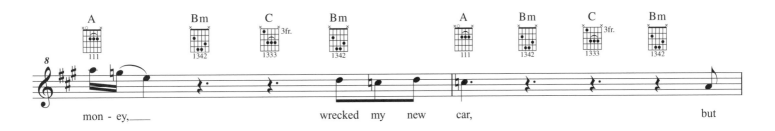

mon- ey,___ wrecked my new car, but

now she's with one o' my good-time___ bud-dies. They're drink-in' in some cross-town bar.___ Some-times I

Chorus:

feel,___ some-times I feel like I been

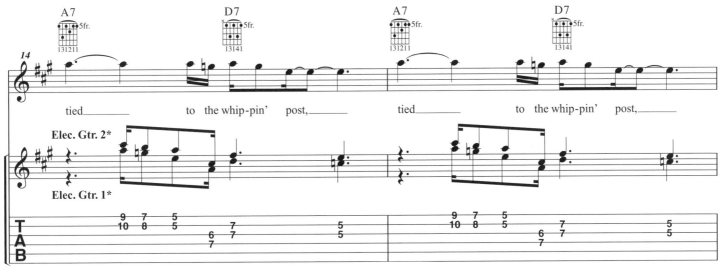

tied___ to the whip-pin' post,___ tied___ to the whip-pin' post,___

*Divisi: Elec. Gtr. 1 plays lower notes/lower string in TAB,
Elec.Gtr. 2 plays upper notes/upper string in TAB.

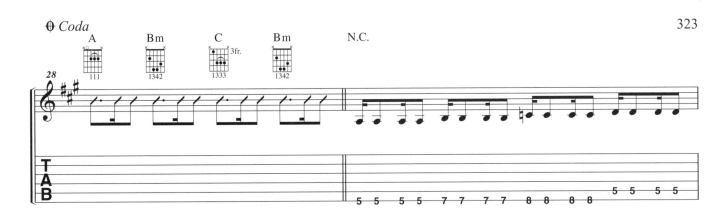

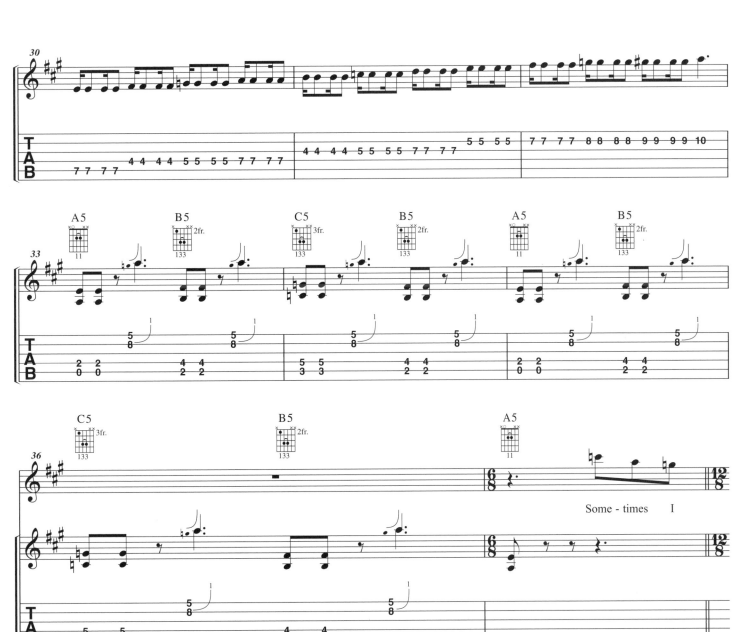

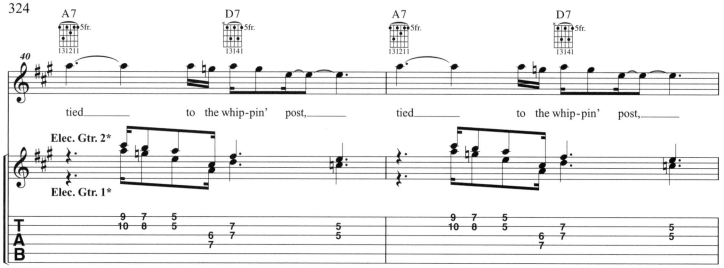

*Divisi: Elec. Gtr. 1 plays lower notes/lower string in TAB,
Elec.Gtr. 2 plays upper notes/upper string in TAB.

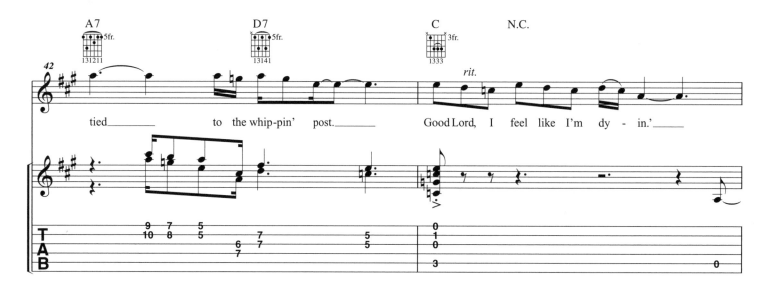

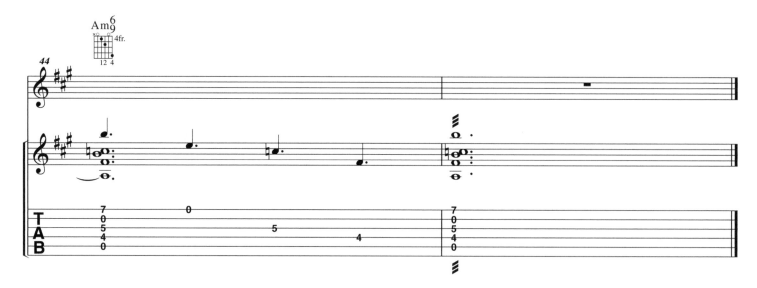

Verse 2:
My friends tell me that I've been such a fool.
And I had to stand back and take it, baby, all for lovin' you.
I drown myself in sorrow, as I look at what you've done.
But nothin' seems to change, the bad times stay the same and I can't run.
(To Chorus:)

YOU CAN'T ALWAYS GET WHAT YOU WANT

Words and Music by
MICK JAGGER and KEITH RICHARDS

Moderately slow ♩ = 82
(gradual accelerando throughout to ♩ = 96 at fade)

Intro:

You Can't Always Get What You Want - 7 - 1

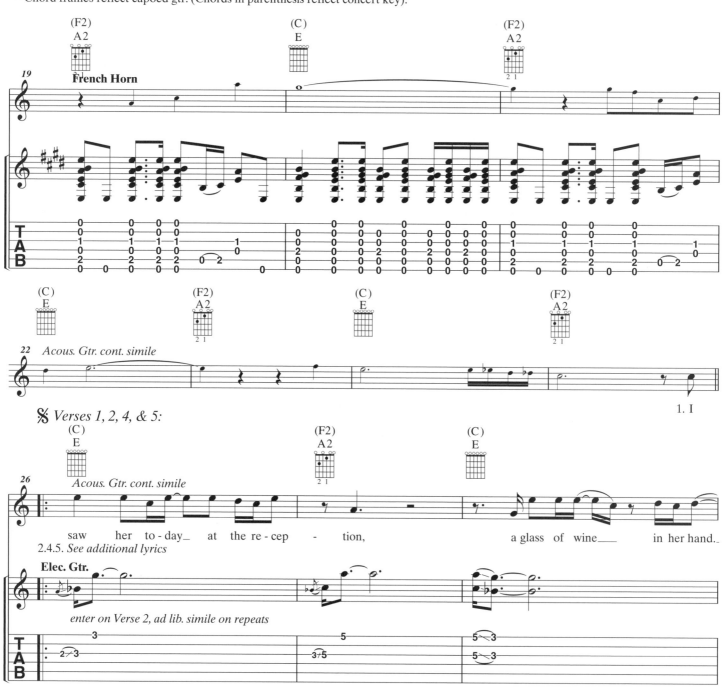

*Acous. Gtr. capo VIII, in Open E tuning: ⑥= E; ⑤= B; ④= E; ③= G♯; ②= B; ①= E
(Chord frames and TAB numbers relative to capo.)
**Chord frames reflect capoed gtr. (Chords in parenthesis reflect concert key).

*Elec. Gtr. in standard tuning w/o capo (TAB numbers are as written).

Moderately ♩ = 90

Verse 3:

went down___ to the Chel-sea drug - store to get___ your___ pre-scrip-tion

You Can't Always Get What You Want - 7 - 4

WHOLE LOTTA LOVE

Words and Music by
JIMMY PAGE, ROBERT PLANT,
JOHN PAUL JONES, JOHN BONHAM
and WILLIE DIXON

Verse 2:
You've been learning, and, baby, I been learning.
All them good times, baby, baby, I've been yearning.
Way, way down inside, honey, you need.
I'm gonna give you my love.
I'm gonna give you my love.
(To Chorus:)

Verse 3:
You've been cooling, and, baby, I've been drooling.
All the good times, baby, I've been misusing.
Way, way down inside, I'm gonna give you my love.
I'm gonna give you every inch of my love.
I'm gonna give you my love.
(To Chorus:)

WILD HORSES

The things_____ you_____ want - ed_____
Now you_____ de - cid - ed_____
I have_____ my_____ free - dom,_____

I bought_them____ for____ you._____
to show_ me____ the____ same._____
but I don't_ have____ much____ time._____

Grace - less
No____ sweep-ing
Faith_ has been

Elec. Gtr. cont. simile

la - dy,____
ex - its____
bro - ken,____

you know_____ who I am.
or_____ off - stage lines
tears_____ must be cried.

You know_ I____ can't_
could make_ me____ feel_
Let's_ do____ some_

____ let____ you
____ bit - ter,
____ liv - ing

slide_ through my____ hands.____
or treat____ you un - kind.____
af - ter we____ die.____

Elec. Gtr.

Wild Horses - 4 - 2

WISH YOU WERE HERE

Words and Music by
ROGER WATERS and DAVID GILMOUR

Slow ♩ = 60   ％ *Intro:*

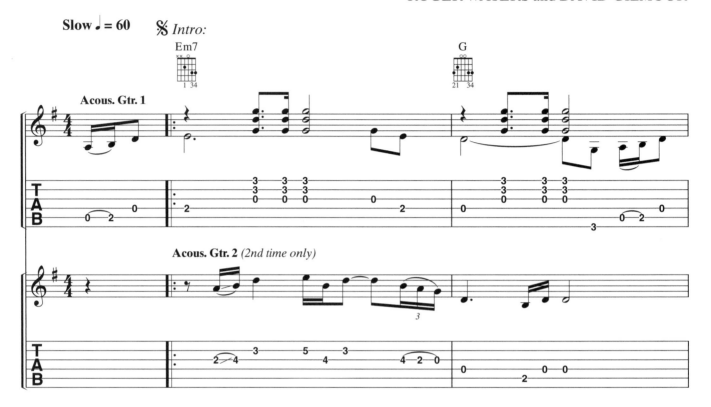

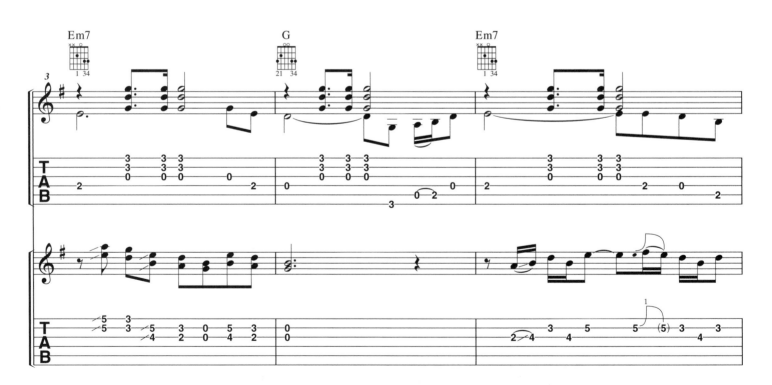

Wish You Were Here - 4 - 1

Verse 2:
How I wish,
How I wish you were here.
We're just two lost souls
Swimming in a fish bowl,
Year after year.
Running over the same ground,
What have we found?
The same old fears,
Wish you were here.

CONTENTS
Ranked by Rolling Stone® Magazine's "The 500 Greatest Songs of All Time"